Praise for the Book

Thoughtful synagogue leaders, both lay and professional, have read books and attended conferences about creating and nurturing synagogues that will lead to a thriving, meaningful Jewish way of life. Hayim Herring's book takes us beyond all the learning we have done so far to new questions. Herring asks exactly what I need to know: Can the mission of my synagogue be framed and shared in such a way that it will find an authentic place in the everyday lives of congregants? Can I challenge preconceptions about the very mission of my synagogue? In pursuit of my goal to create a synagogue that is influential in people's Jewish lives, Herring provides real examples, accessible theory, and concrete suggestions.

—Paula Mack Drill, Orangetown Jewish Center, Orangeburg, New York

Hayim Herring articulates the core changes that must occur for Jewish communities to work most effectively. I would suggest that if one substituted the word "synagogue" with nearly any Jewish agency or organization, many of the same principles that Herring has written would apply. All parts of the Jewish community have to change significantly, and the "rules of engagement" must be rewritten... now.

—Allan Finkelstein, president and CEO,
Jewish Community Centers of North America

Change in our world is no longer incremental but exponential. Every institution must respond to the realities of the modern world, and the synagogue is no exception. The synagogue, while continuing to offer fundamental Jewish values, will be communicating and delivering these key messages vastly different in 21st century. While change at this level can be frightening, it is imperative for the survival of the synagogue. Rabbi Herring inspires us to see how exciting this change can be. He breaks down the walls of fear by imagining a synagogue that is flexible and creative in meeting its challenges. It makes me want to roll up my sleeves and get to work.

—Marcia Zimmerman, senior rabbi, Temple Israel, Minneapolis

One does not have to agree with all the points in this book to see that Rabbi Herring is an exceedingly keen observer of both the external and internal trends that powerfully affect the Jewish community. Readers from all backgrounds within the Jewish community—lay leaders, organizations and the rabbinate—will find ideas and material in this important work that should be thoughtfully considered as our community envisions its future. We ignore Rabbi Herring's observations at our own peril.

—Joseph S. Ozarowski, Jewish Healing Network of Chicago and Visiting Rabbi, Congregation Darchei Noam, St. Louis Park MN

After exploring the challenges facing the American synagogue with vigor and clarity, *Tomorrow's Synagogue Today* provides fresh and creative avenues for rethinking what congregations should be doing. Herring gives concrete examples, suggests new ways for training rabbis and considering rabbinic careers, and provides practical suggestions that can help any synagogue.

—David Teutsch, Louis and Myra Wiener Professor of Contemporary Jewish Civilization; chair, Department of Contemporary Jewish Civilization; director, Levin-Lieber Program in Jewish Ethics

Reading Rabbi Hayim Herring's *Tomorrow's Synagogue Today* gave me hope for religious life in the times to come. Too often we are staid and rigid in our conceptions of the ways we organize ourselves, and unimaginative in the application of our faith. Herring helps us to loosen up and get creative. Insightful and sharp in its analysis, this book offers us a glimpse into what life could be like as faith communities seek to follow the Creator in seeking peace, justice, and wholeness in the world.

—Landon Whitsitt, author of *Open Source Church: Making Room for the Wisdom of All*

The synagogue members of today and tomorrow are Gen Xers, Millennials and Gen Z, whose lives are organized in fundamentally different ways than how many synagogues operate today. Synagogue leaders must align their congregations with these generations, whose understandings of hierarchies and collaboration, native use of technology, and desire to play an active role in producing their own realities are already having a profound impact on the Jewish community, and synagogues in particular. Herring's big vision and practical knowledge of synagogue life unite here to provide the roadmap and insights to help leaders steer their congregations from here to there.

—Lisa Colton, president, Darim Online

Dynamic services, inspiring rabbis, engaged congregants, increasing memberships: these can be accomplished through reenvisioning and reenergizing the congregation. No matter what your religious persuasion, this book has good practical advice about how to accomplish these goals. It shows how, in an electronically connected world, the synagogue can become more inclusive, nurturing, and meaningful. For those who care about the future of the synagogue, I highly recommend this book.

—Alfred A. Marcus, professor and Spencer Chair in Strategy and Technological Leadership, University of Minnesota, Carlson School of Management

Rabbi Herring provides an extremely thoughtful consideration and analysis of the challenges that confront the institution of the American synagogue and its rabbinical and lay leaders in view of current technological, demographic, societal, and cultural realities and trends. *Tomorrow's Synagogue Today* is a most reflective book that is "must reading" for all persons striving to create the institutional frameworks that are necessary to meet the ongoing spiritual and communal needs of American Jews in the 21st century.

—David Ellenson, president, Hebrew Union College-Jewish Institute of Religion

Hayim Herring has distilled years of experience as a successful congregational rabbi, a leading student of institutional change, and an expert in American religion and Jewish life into what is the definitive book on synagogue transformation. Wise, insightful, truthful, and prescriptive, *Tomorrow's Synagogue Today* is a "must read" for anyone interested in reimagining the synagogue in the early 21st century.

—Irwin Kula, president, Clal-The National Jewish Center for Learning and Leadership

Tomorrow's Synagogue Today is a bold, gutsy look at the North American synagogue. Rabbi Herring raises radical questions, most importantly asking if synagogues are doing the right work. He lays out an audacious and compelling vision for synagogues, with boundaries and roles fundamentally different from what we know today. But the book is not pure rhetoric. A set of scenarios concretize the vision and take the reader from the big idea down to the details of a reimagined synagogue. By the time we are through reading, we have the sense that radical change is indeed possible.

—Amy L. Sales, associate director and senior research scientist, Cohen Center for Modern Jewish Studies, Brandeis University

Rabbi Hayim Herring is one of those rare people who can simultaneously observe acutely, manage wisely, and innovate creatively. Herring uses all of those gifts as he invites us to capture a vision in *Tomorrow's Synagogue Today*. Herring's wisdom provides a practical and entrepreneurial guide to forming vibrant, relevant synagogue life.

—Carol Howard Merritt, author of *Tribal Church* and *Reframing Hope*

Hayim Herring's new volume adds immeasurably to our understanding of what it takes for synagogues to reinvent themselves into engaging institutions that exist at the center of people's lives. Herring offers a nuanced, thoughtful reimagining of synagogues, based on a clear assessment of the larger forces—demographics, technology, grassroots movements—that shape how vibrant spiritual communities are developed and maintained. He provides a vision of synagogues based on big ideas and collaborative relationships—and clearly articulates the leadership practices of rabbis and congregants necessary to enact that vision. The book contains just the right blend of theory and practice, offering a valuable guide to the creation of the most vibrant synagogues.

—William A. Kahn, professor of organizational behavior, Boston University School of Management, and coauthor of *This House We Build*.

Tomorrow's Synagogue Today

Tomorrow's Synagogue Today

Creating Vibrant Centers of Jewish Life

Hayim Herring

The Alban Institute
Herndon, Virginia

The Alban Institute
2121 Cooperative Way, Suite 100
Herndon, VA 20171

Scripture references are from *JPS Hebrew-English Tanakh: The traditional Hebrew text and the new JPS translation*, 2000 ed., Philadelphia: Jewish Publication Society

Cover credits:
Eternal light designers/artists: Michael Berkowicz and Bonnie Srolovitz-Berkowicz; eternal light fabrication: Presentations Gallery Ltd., Mt. Vernon, NY
Cover photo: Marcie Ward (Synagogue: Temple Israel, Orlando, FL)
Cover design by Tobias Becker, Bird Box Designs
Author photo by David Sherman

Library of Congress Cataloging-in-Publication Data

Herring, Hayim.
Tomorrow's synagogue today : creating vibrant centers of Jewish life / Hayim Herring.
p. cm.
Includes bibliographical references.
ISBN 978-1-56699-426-2
1. Synagogues--United States--Organization and administration.. 2. Judaism--United States. 3. Judaism--21st century. 4. Rabbis--Office. 5. Leadership--Religious aspects--Judaism. 6. Spiritual life--Judaism. I. Title.
BM653.H47 2012

296.6'5--dc23

2011052213

12 13 14 15 16 VP 5 4 3 2 1

Contents

Foreword

Food shows seem to be everywhere these days, proliferating the airwaves and other entertainment outlets. People love to watch both professionals and amateurs compete and concoct. It is an American obsession. So I have a recipe for you: What do you get when you take one part congregational rabbi, one part not-for-profit leader, and one part scholar, mix in visionary and a liberal sprinkling of mensch, flavor with a sense of humor, sprinkle with wisdom and compassion, and top with a rich layer of accessible teacher? Answer: Rabbi Hayim Herring.

I've had the privilege to know and work with Rabbi Herring over the last decade. He is that rare combination of all the ingredients listed above. I have watched him lead STAR (Synagogues: Transformation and Renewal) and turn it into a cutting-edge organization that has affected the lives of thousands of synagogues across North America. I have worked with him to create programs that have challenged rabbis at all stages of their sacred work to dream big dreams on behalf of the Jewish people and the communities they serve. I have read his blog and his thought-provoking articles. I have participated with him on panels and think tanks and watched him teach and preach. His messages have uplifted me and have challenged my own thinking about what is possible. Somehow—and I am in awe of how well he does this—Hayim gets what is but also sees what could be, and then shares it with his "audience" in ways that are inspiring yet not threatening. That is a rare genius!

And now he has written this book, which I cannot wait to share with my own leadership. I am certain it will become an essential work for any synagogue or religious leader who shares his love and passion, as well as his concern about the future of what we do and bring to our world. Make no mistake about it, as Rabbi Herring will make clear in these pages, religious institutions are challenged today as never before. In the Jewish world, today's shift may be as great as the one that occurred almost 2,000 years ago, when we moved from a centralized sacrificial cult led by hereditary priests to a democratic synagogue focused on prayer and study, and led by scholars who came to be called "rabbis."

Tomorrow's Synagogue Today: Creating Vibrant Centers of Jewish Life invites us to follow a very clear path. Rabbi Herring begins by describing the broader context of U.S. life in the twenty-first century. He reminds us that synagogues and other nonprofits do not exist in a vacuum; rather, these institutions are affected by the same societal realities that affect us all. Next, the book takes us on an "imagining journey" as to what the synagogue of the twenty-first century could look like. I witnessed Rabbi Herring do this visioning work with the leadership of my own synagogue, and the excitement and creativity in the room was palpable. One of Hayim's most visionary pieces rests in his notion of collaboration. An advocate for appropriate collaboration long before the term became popular, Rabbi Herring helps us consider what synagogues might look like if they moved from the mindset of competitor to collaborator, as well as the impact they might have for our communities. Rabbis are still an important piece of the synagogue mix, so our author explores what all this might mean to the changing role of the rabbi in this century. And finally, Rabbi Herring points us in the direction of what this work might look like if we have the courage and foresight to take it on.

Charles Darwin contended that every species must evolve or else it will cease to exist. Rabbi Herring applies this notion to the world of the synagogue and to other institutions that work for the betterment of humankind. But he does more than that. He lays out a blueprint, a roadmap, dare I say a recipe we can all follow, adding our own spices in order to fashion a delicious community that can nourish and sustain us, our children, and our grandchildren well into the twenty-first century. In the end Rabbi Herring offers us a hopeful vision for a reimagined, revitalized synagogue life that will invite and engage us all.

We all owe him a debt of gratitude for feeding us so well.

Rabbi Terry Bookman
Spiritual Leader, Temple Beth Am, Miami, Florida
Cofounder, EITZAH: The Center for Congregational Leadership

Acknowledgments

Since 1984, when I was ordained from rabbinical school, I have benefitted greatly from many Alban Institute publications and resources. I never imagined then that I would be privileged to author a book under the Alban imprint. I hope the five people with whom I've had the most contact at Alban—Richard Bass, Alban's director of publishing; Kristy Pullen, an editor who worked at Alban when I submitted an early draft of my first several chapters; Doug Davidson, who copyedited this book; Lauren Belen, who handled its production; and Beth Gaede, acquisitions editor at Alban—do not mind if I refer to them as menschen (the plural form of mensch), a Yiddish word that roughly translates as "good, caring, and understanding." They are all that and more. I want to especially thank Beth, an exceptional editor, who elevated the level of my thinking and writing with her gentle but insistent touch throughout this process.

I also experimented with vetting some ideas through my blog, Hayim's Blog, which was called Tools for Shuls in an earlier iteration. Those who commented with regularity included Rabbi Daniel Alter, Lisa Colton, Monique Cuvelier, Rabbi Jim Egolf, Elliot Forchheimer, Jordan Goodman, Rabbi Fred Greene, Dr. Maury Hoberman, Larry Kaufman, Fred Passman, Rabbi Neal Loevinger, Rabbi Jason Miller, Rabbi Kerry Olitzky, "Rivster" (the name that appeared in the signature line of comments), Rabbi Jason Rosenberg, and Rabbi Elyse Wechterman.

Over the years, I have learned a tremendous amount about organizational dynamics, social media, and continuing education for rabbis from a group of close colleagues and friends and their thinking permeates this volume. Thank you to Rabbi Terry Bookman, Elana Centor, Jill Friedman Fixler, Gil Mann, Dr. William Kahn, Marsha Rothpan, Gary Stern, and Rabbi Liza Stern for enriching me with your wisdom and your friendship. I also wish to acknowledge Preston Neal, a consultant at Herring Consulting Network, for reviewing a chapter of the manuscript.

In conducting research for this book, I interviewed the following rabbis: Sharon Brous (IKAR, Los Angeles), Tirzah Firestone (Nevei Kodesh, Boulder, CO), David Ingber (Romemu, New York), Asher Lopatin (Anshe Sholom, Chicago), Roly Matalon (B'nai Jeshurun, New York), Rachel Nussbaum (Kavanah Cooperative, Seattle), Micha'el Rosenberg (Fort Tryon Jewish Center, New York), Jonathan Rosenblatt (Riverdale Jewish Center, New York), Danny Zemel (Temple Micah, Washington, DC), and Marcia Zimmerman (Temple Israel, Minneapolis). I know what your schedules are like, and I thank you for your availability and, even more important, your inspirational ideas. Thanks also to Lisa Maloney—these interviews would not have taken place without your administrative assistance.

There are many more rabbis and other Jewish professionals to whom I am indebted from my earlier work at STAR (Synagogues: Transformation and Renewal). Although you are too numerous to mention, I hope each of you knows how much I admire the work that you quietly do for the Jewish community every day. One rabbi whom I will single out as my rabbi and mentor is Kass Ableson. He was my first teacher about the real world of synagogues and is the most amazing exemplar I know of what it means to be a rabbi.

This book has been a family project. My son, Avi Herring, coauthored chapter 5 with me and edited the entire manuscript. His wise perspectives on the Jewish community made every aspect of this book better. My daughter, Tamar Herring, who is also my favorite administrative assistant, always seemed to know when and how to lift my spirits after a hard day of writing. My wife, Terri Krivosha, who after thirty-one years of marriage still helps me in everything that I do, was my mainstay in writing this book and graciously proofread the completed manuscript.

I lovingly dedicate this volume to Terri, to my son and daughter-in-law, Avi and Shaina, and to my daughter, Tamar.

Introduction

Do we need another book on reenvisioning synagogues? That's a legitimate question—and one I asked myself before writing this book. After all, in the past decade many intelligent people who care deeply about synagogues have written about them. So how is this book different from all other books?

A general review of the literature on synagogues suggests that two basic approaches have saturated our thinking, one descriptive and one prescriptive. The descriptive writings focus primarily on the weaknesses of current synagogues and feature words like *market-driven, tribal, elitist, corporate, static, functionary, antiquated,* and *exclusive.* The prescriptive writings offer ideas for infusing synagogue life with greater purpose, building on terms like *welcoming, empowered, spiritual, sacred, communitarian, learning, participatory, healthy, visionary,* and *innovative.*

Both descriptive and prescriptive approaches have helped expand the range of strategies available for synagogue renewal. However, the writings in both categories implicitly take the overall mission of the synagogue as a given, and their recommendations around structure are really about incremental change.[1] In times of overall organizational health, such incremental change is sufficient; but that hardly describes our time, when many synagogues are in a precarious state.

This volume is neither descriptive nor prescriptive, although it includes some elements of each approach. Rather, it is exploratory, in that it stimulates the reader to discover new pathways that will unleash the power of synagogues to exponentially influence people's Jewish lives. Toward that end, I provide several scenarios about what synagogues and the rabbinate could become—not because I believe every synagogue should look this way, but because scenarios stimulate our imaginations about possibilities that are hard to envision within the constraints of daily reality. Additionally, I have interviewed ten rabbis from across the country who are helping to point the way to new models of synagogue mission, governance, and organization.

Today, many people feel a rupture between the relevance of synagogue Judaism and the large and small concerns of their lives. Can we reshape our synagogues so that more people will respond affirmatively to the question, "Do the missions of the synagogue need to be modified so that it strikes a more positive chord with my daily life?" Can our theologians, thinkers, and practitioners find language and concepts that support participation both in a particular Jewish community and in a global world with universal values, so that people who identify as Jews can celebrate what is unique in their heritage while still connecting seriously to the broader world? That is what I mean by a *modified mission* for synagogues.

Are we also ready to create *alternative organizational structures* in congregations? By *alternative structures,* I am referring to how synagogues are organized to do their work.[2] Do their structures impede or facilitate their missions? Do they invite the involvement of a more diverse set of people with new ways of experiencing Jewish life, or do our synagogue cultures actually drive people away, despite our stated intentions of greater outreach? These kinds of questions are especially critical at the board level. In more than twenty-five years of working within the Jewish community, I have learned there is a correlation between high-functioning boards and effective synagogues. If you have an average board, then you can expect an average institution at best.

These modified missions and alternative structures are urgently needed now. I believe that if we do not provide them, our synagogues will experience a tidal wave of change that will wash over them and leave them drowning. This claim rests on my observing the experiences of many industries once considered "too big to fail," such as the automotive, publishing, and entertainment businesses, some of which only survived because of significant government bailouts. When these industries as they'd existed began to collapse, it seemed swift. Yet, with the proverbial wisdom of hindsight, we can now trace the trajectory of changes over a period of time that culminated in their disintegration. The phenomenon of "i-control"—that is, giving consumers significant involvement in decision-making once reserved for company management, such as decisions about products and services—combined with the Internet and enabling technologies of social media, led to massive changes in these industries. Reflect, for a moment, on the implications for companies when consumers become co-producers, comarketers, cocreators, and codirectors! We now understand that these phenomena caused many casualties and left some bruised survivors who are now scrambling to rebuild their industries and professions. The same phenomena are at work in the synagogue.

I hope this book will contribute to developing fundamentally different ways of reconceptualizing the synagogue, so synagogue supporters can avoid this situation. I have written it for the many people who are passionate about the social, educational, financial, spiritual, and volunteer capital within congregations and, more generally, for those who believe that all Jewish community organizations need to be working well in order to maintain a dynamic Jewish life. I believe synagogues can become places of greater inspiration and impact for Jews and non-Jews by undergoing a process of reinventing themselves, as other long-standing institutions have had to do, while still maintaining their integrity. Rather than intensifying anxieties about the future, this volume will hopefully empower more synagogues to take some risks and change the synagogue status quo.

I have structured the book in a logical progression so that each chapter builds upon those before it. In the first chapter, I recall how synagogues functioned prior to the advent of computing and social media technologies. That look back sets the context for chapter 2, which presents a scenario for a contemporary twenty-first century synagogue. This scenario is not a prescription for what every synagogue should look like, but an effort to stretch the imagination about how more synagogues could become vibrant centers of Jewish life and how congregational leaders can chart a new course toward achieving that goal. We will discover that collaboration is a key strategy for expanding the vitality of synagogues as hubs and sponsors of Jewish life. Therefore, chapter 3 focuses on ways synagogues might collaborate with one another, with other Jewish institutions both locally and globally, and with organizations outside the Jewish community. This chapter also explores the limits of collaboration. Chapter 4 describes how the rabbinate is undergoing structural change, asking what future roles rabbis might play and how rabbis might begin preparing for that future now. Chapter 5 furthers that conversation, building on findings from interviews with ten rabbis who have helped forge a path for new models of synagogues. The book concludes with recommendations about the kinds of investments that we who care about synagogues and the Jewish future need to make to ensure that synagogues will remain relevant in shaping Jewish lives and empowering the Jewish community.

Futurist Joel Barker says, "You can and should shape your own future; because if you don't someone else surely will."[3] In that spirit, this book is written as an invitation for you to journey into the synagogue of the future. More than that, it is meant to inspire you to create even more vibrant centers of Jewish life by building tomorrow's synagogue today.

Chapter 1

The Changing Context of American Synagogue Life

Technology's impact on society is indisputable and accelerating. While it might sound like the title of a new television crime show, the term *BIPC*—before internet and personal computing—refers to a time not long past. Yet over the last three decades, new information and communication technologies have transformed our ways of interacting with all kinds of organizations.

Different generations experience the impact of these technologies in various ways. I will explore this in greater detail later, but in brief, technology has rendered the hierarchical "command and control" approach to organizations irrelevant to younger generations. Boomers often have difficulty adapting to this relatively new institutional environment. Even those who have a good grasp of technology do not necessarily understand its vast organizational implications in terms of transparency, fluidity, and the expectation of more rapid organizational response to constituent demands.

Conversely, we find that Millennials and Gen Xers (and we'll see this even more with Gen A, those who cannot remember life before smart phone apps) do not need to transition to these changes in organizational life. These technologies are simply the reality of their daily lives. But when they encounter Jewish institutions mired in the last century's mode of operation, they frequently bypass them. They conclude that if an institution is organizationally out-of-step with them, then it can't be all that relevant.

To better understand how these contemporary realities have changed synagogues, let's set the calendar back to 1985 BIPC I'd just started working in a synagogue that was rightfully proud of its one computer. I was warned not to touch it because I might "break it" (which only made me think, "I can't wait to get my hands on it"). Shortly after I arrived in that congregation, and increasingly through the late 1980s to about the mid-1990s, I began to feel the impact of the first wave of technological change, which was characterized by more widespread adoption of personal desktop computing. Individual computers were just starting to be networked, and Internet-powered social networks were not even on the horizon. But these rudimentary networks created the basis for the deeper social and cultural change that we are experiencing now.

In the BIPC era, different rules governed the Jewish playing field. The guidelines were clear cut, hierarchical, and patrolled by those at the top of Jewish organizations. While the differences between BIPC and the present are vast, a few of them are outlined below.

Hierarchy and Authority

Although social networks existed prior to the launch of the Internet, they were very different. For example, I was part of a local network of congregational rabbis from different Jewish denominations who would meet monthly. We would exchange ideas, try to establish community norms on which we could all agree, and periodically offer jointly sponsored programs. Local Jewish educators seemed to have an even more robust network. But there were no universally accessible social media sites, like Facebook or Twitter, to dramatically power social change.

As a result, the real action took place within the bricks and mortar of the synagogue. The structure of most congregations was hierarchical, with the rabbi sitting at the top of the organizational pyramid. (Fortunately for the congregation I served, the senior rabbi who led the congregation did so with a generous spirit and with an intentional effort to cultivate volunteer leadership.) The rabbi ruled the realm of ritual practice, and the cantor was in charge of Jewish music and arts. Staff members played a central role in all synagogue programs—either introducing big ideas to committees or, when committee members presented their ideas, having a large role in shaping them. If individuals in the congregation had strong preferences for other kinds of religious practice or liturgical music, they had one option—join another synagogue.

While the senior rabbi at my congregation was a consistent advocate for making Jewish knowledge and practice widely accessible, and the cantor used the latest technologies of the time to teach congregants synagogue skills, most, if not all, Jewish education was dependent upon the religious and educational staff. If individual congregants wanted to increase their Jewish knowledge, they had to check a book out from the synagogue or local Jewish library or attend classes on topics determined by the synagogue staff. The channels for broad access to Jewish education simply did not exist.

Restrictive Definitions

In my congregation, which was affiliated with the Conservative movement, membership was available only to Jewish individuals through matrilineal descent or a legally valid conversion. In other words, when a married household consisted of a Jewish person and someone who was not Jewish, the synagogue listed only the Jewish person in the membership directory and addressed congregational mail only to the Jewish person. That was true even if the person who was not Jewish was the family's sole income earner and paid the synagogue dues. Many other populations were similarly invisible to the congregation: gay and lesbian Jews, Jews with disabilities, and single Jews. (Much to the credit of this congregation, there was an active group of Jews in recovery from alcohol and chemical addiction.) Nearly all congregations energetically engaged in this kind of boundary setting, although the Reconstructionist and Reform movements were more interested in expanding the possibilities of non-Jewish participation, while the congregational arm of the Conservative movement sought to maintain minimal involvement of non-Jews.

Clearer Division of Labor

In the not too distant past, there was also a "gentleman's agreement" about how the work of synagogues was distinct from that of other Jewish nonprofit organizations. Synagogues offered Jewish education, prayer services, social justice and Israel-related programs, and life-cycle services for members. But they did not typically offer health, fitness, or recreational programs; these were in the domain of Jewish Community Centers, which are functionally like the YMCAs of the Jewish community (although membership is open to all people, regardless of ethnicity, gender, religion, and sexual orientation). Jewish Federations, the Jewish community's equivalent of the United Way, engaged in major fund-raising for the social welfare needs of the local Jewish community, for Israel, and for distressed Jewish communities in other parts of the world, but typically would not allocate funds for Jewish education within synagogues. When synagogues, Jewish Community Centers, or federations crossed into the other organizations' agreed-upon program areas, the offending institution heard from the aggrieved party or parties.

To summarize, the synagogue I came to in 1985 was much more driven by professional authority and expertise, and was hierarchical, institutionally focused, denominational, and exclusive. This statement is a description and not a judgment. In fact, the congregation I served was healthy and vibrant, progressive in its inclusion of women, and innovative in involving lay leaders in prayer services. Like many other congregations of the era, its model was based on a set of values that was dominant in that day.

And Then the Rules Changed

During the past three decades or so, six societal trends have reshaped many professions in a diverse range of industries. In this relatively short period of time, we have moved

- from the age of organizations toward the age of networks;
- from credentialed professionals toward avocational experts;
- from hierarchical control toward individual autonomy;
- from exclusivity toward inclusivity;
- from monopolization of knowledge toward democratization of knowledge;
- from assuming a fee-for-service economy toward expecting a free-for-service economy (at least at a basic level).

Each of these trends has affected almost every for-profit and nonprofit organization. And as these six individual trends have interacted with one another, they have generated profound, exponential change, shaking the very foundations of organizations.

In organizational terms synagogues have moved from being closed systems to being more open ones. In other words, synagogues are increasingly less insulated from their broader environment and more influenced by their surroundings, even as they have opportunities to change the environments in which they operate. Social media platforms like Facebook and Twitter allow for near-instantaneous communications, and, often, miscommunications. In this environment, synagogue leaders (and other nonprofit leaders) confront intriguing issues that can challenge even their most basic assumptions! Consider the following scenarios, which illustrate a range of challenges attendant to living in an open and dynamic environment.

- As noted earlier, in the prior century, synagogues typically had a monopoly on Jewish after-school education, and other Jewish institutions respected the synagogue's educational turf. Fast-forward to one possible scenario today, in which a significant number of Jewish students attend a competitive, private high school. Some of those students have been participating in the after-school program of a nearby synagogue. With the support of the high school administration, these students and their parents create a Jewish after-school program on site at the high school—a much more convenient option than having to drive to the synagogue.
- A synagogue has no Facebook presence, unlike other local congregations and the nearby spirituality center. So, a well-intentioned congregant creates a Facebook page for the synagogue, featuring congregational events and invitations, photos from a recent family "Shabbat under the Stars" service, and a "Become a Fan of" button. The page is open to everyone—members and nonmembers alike. Coincidentally, the congregant who created the Facebook page is the brother of the congregational president.

- The rabbi of a congregation takes the month of July every summer as her vacation time. Before she leaves town, the rabbi holds a class on the art of giving a sermon, and directs the congregants attending to abundant Web-based commentaries on the weekly Torah portion. Drawing on these commentaries for preparation, a different congregant delivers the weekly sermon each week while the rabbi is away. In August, when the rabbi returns, several congregants ask her if they can continue having congregational members and guests give the sermon at least once a month throughout the year. In addition, they ask the rabbi to offer another workshop on how to give a sermon so that even more congregants can participate in the sermon rotation.
- A large number of guests from other congregations attend a bat mitzvah celebration at a particular synagogue. The parents of the bat mitzvah have been blogging about preparations leading up to the big day, and people on their guest list have been encouraged to share their feelings about the service once it is over. This blog becomes very popular with other families who have an upcoming bar or bat mitzvah, and even develops a small national following. A member of another congregation, whose daughter is approaching bat mitzvah age, is spiritually moved by the ceremony. He posts on the blog, "Your daughter's bat mitzvah helped all of us remember what this ceremony is about. In fact, I'm meeting with your rabbi in a week to find out what I have to do to have my daughter bat mitzvahed at your congregation."
- The community AIDS walk is scheduled on a Shabbat. Although the congregation has participated in the walk previously (when the walk was scheduled on a Sunday), it decides not to participate in this year's walk. A past committee chair of the congregation has a relatively current e-mail distribution list of committee chairs and members.

> She sends an e-mail encouraging those on the list and their friends to attend. She has pasted the congregation's logo on the e-mail and signed the letter, "Past Social Action Chair, Temple Ahava."

These scenarios, although they're made possible by new technologies, do not merely raise technological issues. They raise essential questions about the nature of congregational leadership, structure, and purpose.

As we move into the second decade of the twenty-first century, we are beginning to realize the impact that technology in general and the Internet in particular have had on the most fundamental aspects of our lives and civilization. We understand that technological innovation means change will continue unabated, its pace will quicken, and its impact will deepen. Technology, a midwife to the trends described earlier, has been a powerful catalyst for a thorough rethinking of all institutions—just ask people who've worked for several decades in the fields of entertainment, manufacturing, financial services, and journalism, to name only a few. Each of the trends named above created a ripple of change; together, they have created a tidal wave.

Religious traditions are especially challenged by this new era. Faith traditions do change, but change in them is gradual. Regardless of denomination, faith-based communities are in the business of preservation, transmission, and adaptation. They are entrusted with a heritage that demands continuity, yet also needs to adapt in order to speak to each new generation. Our world of perpetual innovation is particularly difficult for the synagogue because, like most religious institutions, it is resistant to change.

Although religion is not an industry, it experiences the same tectonic shifts that are shaking other fields. Some religious leaders—and I am not referring just to religious extremists—view these forces as an inherent threat to religion. Because religious leaders cannot predict all the ways these cultural and technological shifts will change their faith communities, many are legitimately anxious. One thing is clear to me: While some pockets of religious expression as we know them will continue to exist, religions generally appear ready for a significant reformation. But then again, Judaism and other religions have a demonstrated history of remaking themselves in order to remain relevant to people in each age. In the next chapter, we look at one illustration of how a synagogue might rethink its purpose and structure to better align with today's realities.

Chapter 2

Exploring a Twenty-First-Century Synagogue

How can we fundamentally reimagine a synagogue's mission and structure in an ever-evolving world? This scenario about a fictional synagogue, Temple Torah, helps us think about that big question in new ways by challenging the assumptions we often make about what the work of a synagogue is and how people do that work. Although the temple described in this scenario is fictional, please keep in mind the following ideas as you read about it:

- The scenario may seem futuristic, but the technological infrastructure that it requires can be created today for little or no cost.
- The picture of Temple Torah is not intended as a definitive model that every synagogue should follow. It represents only one springboard to help you think in a fundamentally different way about synagogues.
- Temple Torah is not different because it has an unusually large staff or a hefty operating budget. Rather, it is distinct because its leaders have thought about their work with

> vision, creativity, and openness to new ideas. The concepts below can be scaled to match congregations of all sizes; they require an infusion of creativity, not new capital.

Later in this book, you will read about synagogues that are already doing conceptual work like that of Temple Torah. At some point these organizations decided to experiment with fundamentally new ways of doing their work. I now invite you to experiment with the most relevant parts of this scenario in your own congregation. In doing so, you will expand the number of ways you can think about reframing the purpose and structure of synagogues.

Temple Torah

For the majority of its history, Temple Torah was a dues-paying, affiliated member of the Reform movement. Its orientation and self-perception are still clearly Reform. But several years ago, the national non-Orthodox denominational organizations began allowing congregations affiliated with one movement to pay for a secondary affiliation with another movement and enjoy the benefits of affiliation with the exception of placement services. That change enabled Temple Torah to offer a broader range of programs and services, better suiting its diverse membership. Of course, the congregation has also been adapting resources from other faith communities and the Web.

Recently, Temple Torah revised its mission statement, which proudly proclaims:

> Temple Torah aspires to become a model of a perfected world. You are invited to participate in the temple on your terms, with others who seek to add meaning to their lives and the greater world, by turning this aspiration into a reality.

And its vision statement? It now reads:

> Today, many people perceive that congregational involvement adds little significance to their lives. By transforming the synagogue into a place of ultimate purpose, people now desire to participate in a community that inspires its members with enduring Jewish values. The temple continuously discovers ways to broaden and deepen opportunities for all—young and old, Jewish and non-Jewish, religious and secular, learned and just learning, committed and seeking—so that they use their gifts to make their synagogue a model of a more perfect world.
>
> The congregation is now the Jewish place where people create rewarding connections, renew their minds and spirits, and experience the joy that flows from an intentional community. Every person who invests energy and funds takes pride in being a Temple Torah shareholder and an ambassador to the broader Jewish, religious, and civic community.

This new mission statement was a catalyst for developing a new governance structure. Despite its size, in addition to a board and executive committee, Temple Torah has only three standing committees:

- Nominating
- Finance
- Envisioneering

Envisoneering is a term the congregation coined from the words *envision* and *engineer.* Unlike a strategic-planning process, which typically lasts for up to two years, envisioneering is a flexible process that enables the congregation to gather information in an ongoing way about societal trends and their implications for potential changes within the congregation. A dozen people from within and outside the congregation meet quarterly and share their perspectives on the broader world based on their respective vocations. Committee members include the director of the art museum, a city-council member, a Fortune 1000 senior executive, the CEO of the Jewish Family Service, the rabbi, the temple's executive director, and the chairs of the three standing committees. Members of the envisioneering committee willingly receive training for their positions and in turn are expected to be mentors for others who will eventually replace them.

Clergy and staff members work together in new ways. There are no "departments" (for example, education, youth, and other typical departments) at the temple, because in the past, departments functioned more like "compartments"—communication was inadequate, and clergy and staff passion was underutilized. Today, the board and staff have organized the temple's activity around the three historic, core functions of a synagogue: *beit knesset*, a house of meeting for a variety of activities related to the communal good; *beit midrash*, a house of study and education; and *beit tefilah*, a house of prayer. However, the definitions of these three core synagogue functions have been expanded to include a range of traditional and contemporary experiences and activities that acknowledge a very diverse Jewish community.

Staff members and volunteers are assigned to each of the three core synagogue areas, *beit knesset, beit midrash,* and *beit tefilah.* Together, these groups determine program goals that are aligned with the congregational mission and decide how best to create a multigenerational approach to congregational involvement. As they work within each core synagogue area, these groups reach out to other volunteers to help them on an as-needed basis. They also measure their progress in reaching the established goals. Every few years, staff members rotate areas of focus so that they can continue to develop professionally.

This process of a small group of staff members and volunteers working on each of the core functions of the synagogue, with opportunities for more limited involvement by many additional volunteers, has had many benefits for the synagogue. This planning process

- enables staff and volunteer leaders to make recommendations to the board more easily about what programs to disband and what programs to innovate;
- builds staff and volunteer expertise in particular areas of synagogue life that can then be applied to other areas; and
- positions the synagogue to be more responsive to its members, because it has the capacity to make changes and modifications quickly.

As one example of how this temple functions, let's review how it determines educational programming and instruction. At Temple Torah, the typical adult education and youth education committees have been abandoned. Instead, a small group of staff and volunteers who are knowledgeable about Jewish education are empowered by the board to develop educational profiles of learning for children, teens, and adults—that is, ideally, what a person should know and experience Jewishly throughout the human developmental lifespan. Under the old committee model, educational experiences were fragmented and lacked a holistic approach to thinking about the needs of members throughout their years at the temple. But all that has changed.

This leadership group conducts research about current theories of learning and human development for children, teens, and adults and surveys other congregations for educational ideas. Then, they map out the ideal educational journey they would like each member to experience, from birth through old age. Once they develop these educational profiles, the group convenes additional volunteers to refine the profiles, suggest curricula, and identify ideas and ways to connect learners at different life stages with one another. This group of staff members and volunteers then crafts educational recommendations that are posted on the congregation's website and hosts town meetings to gain valuable feedback from a broader cross section of the congregation. This leadership group meets at the midpoint in the program year to assess the quality of educational programming and make any needed adjustments, and then again at the end of the year to reflect on program evaluation data, which they incorporate into the next year of planning.

What happens when a member has a programming idea that the planning group focused on education has not included? If that member can mobilize a critical mass of individuals who want to pursue the idea, they are welcome to do so, provided that it fits with the educational mission. The congregation will provide facilities and logistical support, although clergy and program staff may not be able to offer much direct help since they are already committed to the educational priorities vetted by the planning process.

The attractive facilities of the temple are heavily utilized for prayer services and social, educational, and recreational programs, but much of the planning work takes place outside the temple. The temple uses current communications and social media tools to make the best use of precious volunteer time and talent. Team members use the Web to communicate logistical information, review documents such as agendas (which are always prepared in advance), minutes, concepts, and feedback. Frequently, these documents are created and edited in an online word processor (like Google Docs) to give all team members the chance to view and edit the same document in real time. In between face-to-face meetings, team members webcast from their laptops or cell phones, and because these technologies still allow team members to see one another, they communicate remarkably well. Those who are unavailable for a particular meeting can at least download the meeting later, since each meeting is recorded and uploaded to the temple's website.

If significant funding is needed to revise programs or implement a new one, the temple has a speedy process to allocate such funds, which are available from an endowed temple incubator fund (one of the many funds within the temple endowment). Board and staff members are always aware of new projects and are available for consultation, but staff members do not serve on all action teams. This enables staff and clergy to maintain a more balanced work schedule.

Members of the clergy are intimately and actively involved in prayer services. They take a key role in making sure that religious services, which are the heart of the congregation's identity, speak to a wide variety of spiritual interests. On any given Shabbat, the temple has at least two services on Friday evening and two on Saturday morning. Of these services, one Friday evening service and one Shabbat morning service follow a standard, established pattern. While some modifications occur in these services, congregants who prefer familiarity to innovation know they can always count on one consistent service on Friday evening and one on Saturday morning.

The other services offer talented congregants opportunities to take an active role in the prayer life of the congregation. In tandem with clergy, they help design, lead, and assess new prayer experiences. What's exciting is that they are not bound by any one prayer book *(siddur)*. Several of the religious denominations license their liturgies and make them available online so that congregations can purchase and download them in a digital format. That way, denominations and congregations have the flexibility to more easily create their own liturgies. Additionally, projects like the Open Siddur Initiative offer a range of liturgies and other resources that can be downloaded and utilized to create a more customized liturgy. Thus, Temple Torah is able to offer two services each week that are more predictable, as well as two other services that are more experimental. There is some overlap among the constituents at each service, but generally the various services attract different crowds. As temple members move through different life stages, they can usually find a service suited to their spiritual inclinations.

Temple leadership understands that liturgical services are among the most public activities of the congregation. So how does the temple ensure experimental services are high quality? The temple solved that problem when a congregant who was a choreographer for the local theater company suggested creating a "lit" (liturgical) lab. Before any new services are offered, and before major modifications are made in existing services, clergy and staff have an opportunity to do a dry run and receive feedback. That way, innovation is encouraged while risk is minimized.

The temple is highly reliant upon volunteers for much of its programming. Therefore, tracking volunteer involvement is a critical staff responsibility. Staff members provide information about volunteer activity to the database expert, who manages a relational database that identifies volunteers by interest area and past volunteer activities inside and outside the temple. The database manager also uses Web analytics to create monthly snapshots of participation rates for key programs. Using information from the database manager, the volunteer coordinator works with staff and board members to offer additional ways for individuals to utilize their talents and grow in their leadership abilities. Since synagogue staff members and leaders are always thinking of ways to enrich the experience of volunteering, volunteers typically rate their experience at the temple as gratifying.

How does the temple fund all its activity? While the temple has a "no-dues" policy, it has a robust fund-development program, which encompasses everything from a healthy endowment fund to *yahrzeit* plaque purchases and the voluntary annual contribution fund. Paradoxically, by abandoning a mandatory dues policy, the temple receives some remarkably large financial gifts. The voluntary dues policy has communicated a clear message that the temple cares deeply about all people, regardless of their financial capacity, and that makes the vast majority of members stretch their financial giving. The voluntary dues policy also helps to communicate a clear message that temple leaders care first and foremost about people developing a relationship with staff and lay leaders.

Additionally, thanks to new legislation, the temple was able to establish a for-profit social enterprise business. Along with the local mosque and church, the temple co-owns a kosher-hallal-vegetarian fair-trade coffee shop named "On Solid Grounds." A percentage of the coffee shop's revenue is donated to the local food shelf, and it has become a place where people of diverse backgrounds and multiple generations mingle and discuss community issues. It's run just as well as any other coffee shop but also has room for interested volunteers.

The temple also has program partnerships with several other Jewish institutions (such as the Jewish Family Service), and also partners with a nearby yoga and wellness center, a cooking school, and the local university, which regularly uses the temple as a satellite site for Jewish studies courses. When volunteers have ideas about new programs for the temple, whether in partnership with another organization or as stand-alone programs, they are encouraged and empowered to develop them and organize them, provided that they fit within the temple's mission.

The temple's public presence is greatly enhanced by a weekly cable show hosted by one of the rabbis, and other clergy members have international followings on their blogs. And you can always tell when members of the temple community are involved in civic activities: someone designed a great logo for the baseball hats and T-shirts temple volunteers wear.

If you just want to check the temple out without visiting, you can experience the temple through its website, where you'll find a virtual "temple tour," webcasts of classes, spirited services (*davenning*), and video clips of current *chesed* projects. Still, if you want a more independent review, you can find information about the temple on Yelp or in the Everything Local website.

Temple Torah owns an apartment in Israel that it rents to individuals at cost, and the temple website features video clips and updates from those who spend time there. Or, if you want to visit Israel or other Jewish communities with friends from the temple, you can take one of the trips it frequently sponsors. While the temple is a significant local institution, it fosters a global relationship with many other Jewish communities through such sponsored trips as well as through lectures and programs about Jewish communities throughout the world.

The temple is a vibrant hub for abundant, purposeful activity. But its leaders also recognize that it is a platform for organizing people to experience and express their Jewish identity on their terms, provided that people work within the temple's mission. Temple leaders are always thinking about how their efforts are changing Jewish lives, supporting people on a deeper journey into Judaism, and strengthening the broader community.

Major Questions

The Temple Torah scenario raises many questions—some more significant than others. Before you continue reading, I want to ask you to stop for a moment and list the questions this scenario raises for you. Below I've listed in no particular order some of the questions I believe are most central.

1. How can synagogue leaders reconfigure the missions and vision of their institutions to better reflect changes in the U.S. Jewish community and the broader society and make the best use of recent technological innovations, while still

remaining faithful to the rich history and legacy of their religious tradition?
2. How can staff and volunteers work together to create governance structures that reflect the new mission and encourage participation and innovation?
3. What is the role of the rabbi in this new institution? How do volunteers and volunteer leaders connect with the synagogue?
4. What do the primary functions of a synagogue—prayer, education, and community building—look like when placed within the alternative model of a synagogue like Temple Torah?
5. How can synagogues collaborate with institutions inside and outside the Jewish community, viewing these organizations not as threats but as potential partners?

Each congregation will answer these questions differently; to be sure, not every reimagined synagogue will look like Temple Torah—nor should it! While these questions can be answered many different ways, what's most important is to seriously consider each of these issues, as I do in the pages that follow.

Moving toward a Twenty-First Century Synagogue

We've already noted that while technology plays a pivotal role in how Temple Torah operates, these new technologies do not drive the temple's creativity. Technology only creates the conditions for a different set of organizational values and actions to emerge. Congregational leaders must exploit the potential inherent in emerging technologies to markedly expand the possibilities of congregational reinvention and vitality.

Broadly speaking, the central leadership challenge today is to help synagogues shift from a closed-source platform to what is often referred to as an open-source platform. The term *open source* refers to computer programs where the source code is available to the general public, which invites free and open collaboration by members of the community. Speaking about congregations as open-source platforms is more than trendy jargon. Rather, by reframing a congregation as an open-source platform, congregational leaders can understand the implications of the sweeping changes underway in our most cherished institutions for congregational life. Gratefully acknowledging the work of five seminal thinkers on culture and social media, Chris Anderson, Jeff Jarvis, Beth Kanter, Alison Fine, and Charlene Li,[1] here is how I understand the meaning and repercussions of thinking of congregations as *open source platforms:*

- Organizations no longer have exclusive control over their message—and that is perhaps one of the most anxiety-producing characteristics of an open-source age. Detractors are free to comment (sometimes unfairly) about an organization—spreading their views through text and video by blogging, tweeting, texting, Facebooking, or plain old-fashioned e-mailing. Organizations have to pay attention to well-meaning supporters as well, who may misrepresent an issue or program. On the other hand, organizations can also benefit greatly from this open environment. When enthusiastic supporters comment freely and publicly about their involvement in an organization, their views have more credibility than those of a paid staff member.
- Almost no information is private, and almost all information is accessible. Therefore, organizations must be transparent about their activities and operations or they will lose the trust of the public.

- When energized by a vision, many people will collaborate generously and voluntarily, cocreating content, activities, causes, products, and events that they find important. "Collaborative cocreation" means that "experts" and "nonexperts," those with official titles and those with no titles all, have equal voices.
- Mistakes happen when nonexperts are coproducers, but when a group of people works together, group members will take responsibility for correcting them.
- An organization's success is tied to its ability to distribute knowledge and leadership. When organizational leaders try to preserve control by sharing information selectively (only with particular people or in certain settings), they limit their ability to draw on the talent of staff and volunteers.
- It is important to think of synagogues as a platform for organizing people with similar interests rather than believing our goal is to manufacture community from the top down. For example, most synagogues could serve as an organizing mechanism for people who have an interest in cooking. The synagogue does not have to "own" that group; it only enables interested people to come together. The synagogue could provide meeting space, recipes, information about kosher and organic food, and other related resources. In doing so, the synagogue can reach people who might otherwise choose not be involved in its activities.
- In a similar vein, synagogues need to move off of their organizational charts—which reinforce thinking only of *existing* committees—and cultivate the art of seeing communities that do not yet exist.
- Often, synagogue leaders implicitly equate *community* with large numbers of people. As social media resources make smaller groups sustainable, synagogues should recognize the importance of niche communities and foster linkages

among them when appropriate. In an environment where people seem to prefer more intimate communities, it is time to relinquish an understanding of *community* that expects everyone in an organization should frequently celebrate together in large crowds.
- It's critical to have 24/7, 365 day-a-year feedback and response mechanisms (through a website, voice mail, e-mail, chat, Twitter, and yes—even "snail mail").
- Organizations should focus on what they do best and network with others to achieve the rest.

Social media are fundamentally changing the central features of organizational life. In light of these forces that are reshaping organizational behavior, each synagogue has the critical task of rethinking its mission and vision, organizational values, governance structures, approach to congregational engagement, cost structure, and use of technology. If synagogues and other nonprofits do not change these defining aspects of their organizations, they run risk of going out of business, as I explain below. We happen to be living in an era of discontinuity with the past, in large measure because of technology. This requires congregational leaders who will generate questions that challenge the fundamental purposes and assumptions of their organizations and then engage in strategic planning that will set their congregations on a new course for a new era.

Mission and Vision

While I have not conducted a formal study of synagogue mission statements, I have reviewed a variety of mission statements from denominational and independent synagogues.[2] In general, many synagogue mission statements emphasize their particular Jewish interests over more global ones. True, these statements may reference phrases like *social justice, tzedek* (righteousness), and *tikkun olam* (repairing the world), but they generally appear to me (and I suspect many others!) to reflect a community that seeks primarily to serve individuals already committed to the same faith. As an exercise in contrast, try searching for the phrase "sample church mission statements." You will see that many Christian churches emphasize bringing their faith to the world. Historically, Judaism has not been an evangelical religion, and I am not suggesting that synagogues work actively to convert non-Jews. However, if synagogues believe they have a serious responsibility to the greater world and that the Jewish religious tradition has an important contribution to make to others, the language of our mission statements and the work we do must reflect this belief. People reading a synagogue mission statement, regardless of their own religion, should understand this is a community engaged in important, purposeful work that affects all. Such mission statements may even inspire non-Jews to learn more about the Jewish community.

Perhaps, then, the next stage in Judaism's evolution is to recalibrate the balance between looking inward and looking outward. In our postmodern age, Judaism needs to make not an either-or but a both-and choice. This means taking Jewish values, traditions, and insights to the public in noncoercive, engaging, and enjoyable ways. That is why the fictional Temple Torah's mission declares that it "aspires to become a model of a perfected world." A synagogue like Temple Torah would operationalize its mission by tackling large issues with Jewish wisdom, developing solutions that can be applied in the temple while also deploying those solutions to local, national, and global faith communities—those that are Jewish and those of other religions.

If Temple Torah really existed, its vision statement—that is, its picture of an ideal future—would need further development. But even in its basic form, it speaks about engagement—with its own congregants, with people from all backgrounds who comprise its community, and with the broader world through the issue of *tikkun olam*, of making the synagogue a microcosm of what a perfected (just, compassionate, egalitarian, learned) world can be. A more detailed version would describe the activities in which the temple would engage to create this microcosm. True to its mission, the synagogue's vision is both particular and universal, and will have special appeal to the generations that have avoided synagogues—Gen Xers, Millennials, and the newest generation, often known as Gen G (for Google) or Gen A (for apps).

Organizational Values

Regardless of whether a synagogue has an explicit values statement, you can recognize an organization's lived values in its culture. An organization's culture includes its implicit and subconscious processes for accomplishing work, and may contrast with the organization's formal structure.[3] In my contact with many synagogues throughout the United States, I have found that the organizational cultures of many congregations are informed with values that date from the early 1970s to the mid-1980s. The challenge facing such synagogues is that many individuals live and work in a culture characterized by a markedly different value set. In the table on the following page, I have tried to contrast these two value sets.

In reviewing these characteristics, you can see how technology has accelerated the widespread adoption of some values from an earlier age (inclusion, egalitarianism) while also giving birth to new values (distributed knowledge, interdependence). The context in which most of us live our lives has fundamentally changed in the past thirty years, but synagogues, for a variety of reasons, have lagged in recognizing this shift.

This table also clarifies why there are generational differences in attitudes toward many existing synagogues. If you are a part

Yesterday's Organizational Values	Contemporary Organizational Values
Authoritarian	Democratic, egalitarian
Hierarchical	Fluid, improvisational
Authority determined by degree and professional training	Influence determined by expertise, passion, and experience
Honor tradition	Respect innovation
Membership based	Community driven
Commitment to institution	Commitment to cause
Self-sufficiency	Interdependence and collaboration
Denominational	Postdenominational
Limited local orientation	Expansive, global orientation
Exclusive	Inclusive
Closely- held knowledge	Distributed knowledge

of the BIPC generation, which includes Baby Boomers (born between 1946 and 1964) and people who are older, you were likely shaped by the values in the left-hand column. On the other hand, those who are Gen Xers (born between 1965 and 1976) and Gen Yers/Millennials (born between 1977 and 2002) tend to be more committed to the values in the right-hand column. Boomers who are trying to make the transition to a new set of values sometimes feel like they have been given a complex piece of equipment with no owner's manual or tech-support. This contemporary set of values is in full play at Temple Torah.

Governance

Governance—the who and how of formal decision making—is problematic in many congregations. Processes for making decisions are sometimes cumbersome or unclear. And, when a group of volunteers follows the approved channels to have an idea approved, but a major donor objects to the outcome and the rabbi or synagogue president then ignores the group's decision, volunteers lose faith in the congregation's governance. Insufficient attention is given to creating a pipeline for volunteer leadership. Board meetings can devote too much time to relatively trivial details (like approving a $500 expense), while major issues like assessing the impact of a key program are ignored. Board members can feel disempowered if they believe staff members are making all the decisions or that the real power lies with an executive committee.

I have seen some exceptions, but my experience is that congregational governance is typically in a dysfunctional state. Congregational boards often focus on operational issues and neglect policy discussions. The process for how key decisions are made is often unclear, and too much decision-making power is concentrated in the hands of one or two individuals. That is why it can be so difficult to attract the high-caliber leaders synagogues need in order to thrive. Fortunately, there are some excellent models of general nonprofit governance and supporting resources available.[4] These resources can help congregations pay attention to how leaders are developed, how and by whom decisions are made, and how they can create simple, transparent ways of working that facilitate sound, innovative, and nimble decision making.

Congregations should consider carefully how many standing committees they really need. Temple Torah has found that it can more easily fill volunteer needs and attract quality individuals if people know they can commit to a project without signing up for a committee. Because the temple has only three standing committees in addition to its governing board, staff members are able to work more closely with each committee that is doing the legally required and organizationally essential governance work of the congregation. Groups that come together to work on specific projects seek to do as much work as possible prior to group meetings so that meeting time can be focused on substantive issues. Such meetings are much more rewarding to staff members and volunteers, and attract future leadership to standing committees.

Creative Use of Staff

Temple Torah's scenario clearly requires a staff of secure and creative synagogue professionals. Staff members know how to disagree with one another over principled issues, but they also relate generously to one another. They appreciate one another's multifaceted personalities, diverse talents, passions, and interests. They support one another in their work, challenge one another to grow individually by taking on new roles, and share what they learn from their continuing educational experiences. With work and ongoing nurturing, synagogue staff members can create this kind of collaborative working environment. In fact, where such collaboration is not the reality, lay leaders and professionals should be asking how they could create it. Why wouldn't staff members want to invest as much energy as possible into making their professional relationships as rewarding and as fulfilling as possible, given the purpose and intensity of their work!

In addition to fostering a collaborative environment, professionals and lay leaders should review how staff time is spent. The following questions can serve as a jumping-off point for this kind of reflection:

1. Are rabbis willing to delegate to volunteers or staff members some of their existing, less essential work so that they can do more of the work they are especially trained to perform?
2. Are boards willing to release their rabbis from attending meetings where their presence really is not needed so that the rabbis can concentrate more on outreach, teaching, and spiritual guidance?
3. Can more Jewish educators utilize digital educational resources in the classroom and empower their students to become more self-directed learners?

4. Are congregations that employ executive directors willing to pay more for those who have experience in managing nonprofit organizations and are Jewishly educated, recognizing that individuals with this kind of background could play a broader role in congregational management?

People are the most important asset of any organization. I've observed many congregations in which staff members are overworked but underutilized. Staff persons invest hours in areas where they have little training, leaving them with insufficient time for areas that require their education and skills. For example, a staff member may be heavily involved in marketing a program, leaving her inadequate time to prepare for adult education classes. While staff should have input into the marketing of their programs, laypeople are often much better qualified to take responsibility for this task.

Much work must be done around staffing issues. A significant step would be for lay leaders and staff members to jointly examine inherited staff functions. Which of those jobs is really a poor use of staff time? Which tasks could be shifted to capable volunteers who, by taking on these tasks, would feel greater ownership of their synagogue lives? Although many staff members recognize that they are overburdened with work, they do not always know how to relinquish it. We see this same paradox in the Torah, when Moses' assistant, Joshua, is threatened by the appearance of two unauthorized prophets, Eldad and Medad. When Joshua suggests that Moses restrain them, Moses replies, "Are you wrought up on my account? Would that all the Lord's people were prophets, that the Lord put His spirit upon them" (Num. 11:25–28). In this instance, Moses teaches his student, Joshua, that effective leaders are generous in spirit, empowering other leaders and not allowing their personal insecurities to limit the need to share in the work.

Appreciating and Respecting Congregants

Often, synagogues take a long time to accomplish a task. While eternity is a hopeful theological concept, it is a frustrating operational principle! Volunteer time is too precious to squander. What needs to be considered when recruiting volunteers for synagogue work, whether for the board, standing committees, or specific projects?

Today's volunteers are in some ways different from those of previous generations. Individuals may still volunteer because someone they respect asks them to do so, to satisfy social needs, to fulfill a religious commandment, out of an altruistic desire to do good in the world or, in the worst cases, because they are made to feel guilty if they do not. But other factors shape whether someone will volunteer for an organization. Many volunteers today look for tasks that have a beginning, middle, and end—or, in the words of a national expert on volunteer engagement, Jill Friedman Fixler, projects that are not a "life sentence."[5] Volunteers want to know how their involvement will make a difference in the congregation and in their own personal lives. They do not want to engage in mindless work; rather, they want to contribute their skills and knowledge or, alternatively, develop other facets of themselves. Volunteers need to know what is expected of them and should be supported appropriately by staff. Additionally, they need to know that any suggestions they have for how a task might be done better are welcome and will not be stifled by staff and other volunteers. If synagogues are going to invite the involvement of volunteers and provide them with a fulfilling experience, then those who are doing the inviting really need to prepare for them.

With that as background, try rereading the Temple Torah scenario. Note that volunteers are used strategically. Preparatory work for a meeting is done, so meeting time is focused on issues that require group thinking and planning. The work volunteers do is meaningful and designed to fit conveniently into their schedules. Note also that it is the task, and not the title of the volunteer or staff person, that drives the work of the congregation. And Temple Torah does not tolerate phrases such as "It can't work" and "We've always done it this way."

But what is a Jewish meeting without schmoozing and noshing? The answer: not a Jewish meeting! Indeed, schmoozing and noshing play an important part in building strong social bonds, and they can simply be fun—which is why we must ensure that our more structured meeting atmosphere still includes opportunities for such social connection. To strike a balance between the business and social aspects of meeting, some organizations will schedule an optional fifteen-minute social time before the official meeting or a brief social break in the middle of a meeting. That balance sends a signal that a congregational meeting is not just any business meeting, but a place where spiritual work and community are developed. In addition, Jewish learning has a permanent place in meetings when it informs discussions and participants respect the time allotted for it.

American Jews are among the most highly educated groups in the United States. What would happen to congregational life if volunteering increased by 10 percent, 15 percent, or even 20 percent? I think we would see a dramatic burst of energy and creativity in congregations, and deeper spiritual and emotional engagement on the part of many more synagogue-goers!

Financing the Synagogue

A common complaint about synagogues is that they are too expensive. Back in 1991, the late Gary Tobin, a farsighted thought leader and researcher of the Jewish community, cautioned that the synagogue dues model was problematic.[6] His words are especially relevant in difficult economic times. Although U.S. Jews are among the most financially successful groups in the country, the expectation that members will pay annual dues of anywhere between $1,000 and $2,500 can be financially daunting for some families. While most synagogues do not turn people away because of financial need, the process that people looking for financial relief must face can feel humiliating. At the same time, there are plenty of people who can afford to pay membership dues but do not for a variety of reasons.

Consider some of the difficulties of the current synagogue membership model:

- Many synagogues are burdened with relatively expensive, aging facilities that are underutilized much of the year. Boomers who retire and move to warmer locations may be willing to pay membership dues to a synagogue in their new, warm-weather community but most do not want to pay for a building fund, which they likely had to do while living in their previous community.
- Rabbinical and cantorial compensation is another major cost. Relative to their education and the demands of their positions, the average salary of rabbis and cantors is not excessive when compared to professionals like doctors, lawyers, and accountants. However, the question is, are these expenses sustainable for the average synagogue?
- Membership retention is a problem. For many Jews, synagogue Judaism is coterminus with child-centered life-cycle events. When children leave, parents drop membership.
- In recent years synagogues have improved opportunities for involving families that do not fit the traditional model of two parents and a couple of children. But we still have a ways to go in increasing membership and involvement of LGBTIQ Jews, single adults, single parents, empty nesters,

and other individuals who form today's Jewish demographic mosaic.

- As others have noted, the financial cost of synagogue membership does not outweigh the perceived value for many people today. Increasingly, even if individuals can afford synagogue dues, the majority of them will only pay for services they use personally and will not support a congregation simply because it is a good cause. Outside of the Orthodox community, the majority of U.S. Jews "use" synagogues little or not at all.[7]
- It is likely that the mindset fostered by the "free" benefits of the Internet has begun to affect attitudes toward paying for the range of services and programs synagogues offer. Chabad, the worldwide Orthodox movement that reaches out to Jews of all backgrounds, has also cultivated that attitude by offering its religious and educational services for free (or for a nominal charge) and relying upon donations to fund its activities. Additionally, Taglit-Birthright Israel, an organization that has provided free educational trips to approximately 300,000 Jewish young adults and seeks to ensure that one of every two Jewish young adults will visit Israel, may inadvertently contribute to a feeling of entitlement. Many younger Jews have experienced this life-changing experience for free, and some will undoubtedly question the expectation that they should pay for the services and programs synagogues offer.
- Religious school and youth activities often require "subsidies" from those who do not have children or do not have children in the religious school. Some families without school-age children are no longer willing to pay for religious schools as a part of their synagogue dues and have started synagogues or minyans that do not have a religious school by design.

So what are some of the options for synagogues to reduce costs so that they can become less reliant upon membership dues and make synagogue membership more affordable? Some congregations may need to explore the benefits of leasing space as opposed to owning a building. A lease can sometimes provide congregations with more financial flexibility than maintaining a property, especially an older building. This is admittedly a tough measure, and I am very sensitive to the intangibles of ownership, but all options deserve consideration when thinking long term.

Other congregations will need to reimagine congregational life with a part-time rabbi (more about that later). Others will have to offer a hard choice to their clergy, either reducing their salary or not renewing contracts. It pains me to publicly raise the issue of compensation. But it is even more painful—and, in my opinion, unethical—to ask a rabbi who has worked for years in a congregation to leave so that the synagogue can hire a "less expensive" rabbi. Congregational leaders and rabbis need to be prepared to have these conversations, just as many employers and employees in other arenas have done.

Strategies for Growth

Cost cutting can only get a congregation so far. Synagogues must think about strategies for growth as well. If synagogues try only to cut their way out of their financial problems, they will downsize their impact on the individuals and communities they serve. Here are several ideas about how congregations can place themselves in a growth mode. Some ideas can be implemented in the short term and others in the longer term.

Congregations can explore creating a for-profit business, as the fictitious Temple Torah did with its coffee shop. The potential for nonprofits to create for-profit entities is not new and not easy, but many temples include both business people who could help and attorneys who understand the legal structures that allow for such ventures. When you think about the number of business-like activities in which synagogues already engage—such as Purim carnivals, gift shops, and annual fund-raisers—starting a for-profit venture is not such a stretch, especially if several synagogues or other nonprofits partner in this venture.

While I have not yet seen corporate sponsorships appear in synagogue life, that possibility deserves consideration as well, provided that sponsors align with the synagogue's values. Could local businesses sponsor the youth group, in the same way they sponsor Little League teams? Many synagogues already seek revenue-generating advertisements in their key communications vehicles, so why not think about expanding existing sources of revenue?

To help lower overhead costs, synagogues should investigate whether partnering with other institutions could create economies of scale or other types of savings. For example, could other Jewish organizations or nonprofits share administrative space with your synagogue? If merging with another congregation is possible, perhaps now is the time to explore it. Or, could two congregations share one facility without formally merging? Jewish organizations in a community might jointly purchase supplies, custodial services, health insurance, energy, and other goods and services that can be handled in a single "back-end" office. All these are viable ways to decrease expenses at a time when funds are tight.

Increased volunteer engagement helps people grow Jewishly while also using their talents to benefit the synagogue. Volunteer time translates into significant contributions to the synagogue. True, greater volunteer involvement creates additional staff needs, but with the empowerment approach Temple Torah takes in allowing volunteers a more active role in shaping the congregation, staff needs can be minimized. Increasing volunteer involvement can reward both the individual and the institution.

As noted earlier, while some individuals and families must struggle to pay minimal synagogue dues, others are easily able to contribute above the "fair-share" level. As a Boomer who also has many Boomer friends, I believe people of my generation often feel a sense of disengagement from congregational life, even though people's search for meaning often heightens in later years. When congregations engage Boomers, they can tap into their experience, financial resources, and desire for involvement in meaningful work. Boomers are an overlooked population and represent a great opportunity for congregations in many ways.[8] Many people my age already have an estate plan or are in the planning process. Therefore, now is the time to be speaking with us, as well as older members with long-time involvement. It does not hurt to remind us of the Jewish value of *tzedakah*, of doing what is just and lending a hand to the generations that will follow, as our elders have done for us.

Of all the strategies mentioned, perhaps the most critical is to reach out to the majority of Jewish individuals and families who are not involved in synagogues. In some cases declining Jewish populations make that impossible, but in many more, demographics actually favor outreach to Jewish individuals and families who are not synagogue members. The actual percentage of Jewish individuals who affiliate with a synagogue in any U.S. community is significantly lower than the potential. If your area's rate of synagogue affiliation is 25 percent, rather than compete with other local congregations for the same 25 percent, why not reach out to the other 75 percent? If more congregations would open their doors widely for outreach, especially to non-Jews who are married to Jewish individuals and to spiritual seekers—the potential for involving vastly more people in synagogues expands exponentially. In addition, reaching out to the uninvolved does not have to come at the expense of neglecting dues-paying individuals. Outreach can actually energize existing members![9]

The possibility of real synagogue growth is not wishful thinking, as the Chabad movement has already shown. Anecdotally speaking, many synagogues seem so beset with the challenges of survival that they do not imagine that growth and outreach are actually possible. But with confidence that growth can increase both revenue and congregational vitality, synagogue leaders will become more creative in finding ways to connect the unaffiliated population with congregational life.

Technology

Just as computer chips are now or soon will be embedded in just about every object, so too can technology be enmeshed in just about every aspect of congregational work. Technology should not be thought of as a separate focus in congregational work but as an integral aspect that allows congregations to extend their reach and deepen their impact. If you are involved in any aspect of synagogue life, here are a few questions that you want to be asking about technology use in a congregation:

1. Does your congregation use online feedback mechanisms, like electronic surveys and a "comment" section on your synagogue website, so that it can respond to concerns and test ideas?
2. Are you able to segment your congregational database by age, zip code, or affinity so that you can be selective about what you communicate to people of different ages and interests? Sending congregants too many e-mails will make them more likely to hit the "spam" button.
3. In addition to recognizing Jewish life-cycle events, is your congregation able to acknowledge congregants on important secular milestones, like birthdays, anniversaries,

and retirements, so that you can relate to them more personally?

4. How do you communicate with members of the congregation who are not technologically adept, like some elderly members who do not have computers or have difficulty making their way through a digital maze?
5. If a twentysomething-year-old looked at your website, what would her reaction be? What about a thirtysomething-year-old, or a fortysomething-year-old? You don't have to guess—just invite feedback from them!
6. To what extent does your congregation match the medium of communications with its intended audience? Conversely, how easy is it for people to find information about the congregation through the congregation's Twitter feed, Facebook page, and voice mail system?
7. Do all of your task forces and committees have "geeks" as members?
8. How does your website support learning and spiritual growth?
9. How does your site promote involvement in congregational activity in general?
10. Can people easily pay membership dues, make contributions, and pay for events? (Some churches make it easy for members to make donation by credit card, even going so far as to provide ATMs, or automatic tithing machines, in church foyers.)

Over the past five years, I have seen improvement in how synagogues are using technology. Still, my impression is that most synagogues do not avail themselves of the power to teach more, connect more, and operate better by embedding technology into their understanding of congregational life.

A Concluding Caution

Many synagogues will need to address these issues quickly or risk running out of funds to effectively fulfill their mission. To use an analogy, Ford Motor Company went through some financially harsh restructuring in 2006, rode through the economic crisis that began in 2007, and shortly thereafter became profitable without the help of government loans. General Motors did not, and the unthinkable happened—it went into bankruptcy and was forced by the government to make the hard choices it had postponed. GM had to restructure amidst tremendous financial stress and not completely on its own terms. The lesson for synagogue leaders amid all this financial turmoil is to make the hard choices now, while you have time, or risk closing your doors. And remember, unlike GM, you might find no one to bail you out.

The good news is that there is still time for synagogues to engage in bold, imaginative action. With the knowledge gained from observing massive disruptions in other industries, we know that radical reenvisioning must replace mere tinkering at the temple. An important component in this reenvisioning process is for synagogues to stop viewing themselves in isolation from other organizations that have overlapping and complementary agendas. That is why in the next chapter I will expand upon a theme in the Temple Torah scenario: collaborations and partnerships with other organizations inside and outside the Jewish community. I treat these topics separately in the next chapter, as they are critical paths to success for synagogues.

Chapter 3

The Case for Collaboration

Any road to synagogue reinvention ultimately leads to collaboration. Why? In this era people value multiple options that can be customized to their tastes, yet no synagogue can achieve excellence in every area. To understand how valuable collaboration can be, think about what it means to try and enjoy all that a Jewish community has to offer. How many synagogues and organizations must one join to take advantage of a broad range of Jewish educational, social, spiritual, and cultural programs and experiences? When synagogues and other organizations collaborate, they have the potential to increase both the quality and the quantity of their programs—attracting more individuals to their varied programs and high quality services.

Initially, collaboration requires more work than going it alone, but it offers opportunities for participant enrichment that individual congregations cannot provide on their own. When synagogues focus more on serving members and less on establishing and maintaining the security and prestige of their individual institutions, they will begin moving off the path of just surviving and on to the road of thriving.

Defining Collaboration

What is *collaboration?* It depends whom you ask. For funders, it can be a code word for a merger. For a program officer, it can mean more work with ambiguous benefits. For a lay leader, it may mean efficiency. For many others, it offers a vision of doing something great that no single person or organization can do alone. In speaking with potential partners about the possibility of collaboration, the first order of business is to develop a shared understanding of what *collaboration* means.

Here is one useful definition of *collaboration:* two or more organizations working together, while retaining their identity and autonomy, in order to provide constituents with a higher level of service than each organization could provide individually. Participants in a collaboration share jointly in the costs and benefits of working together.

Let's use adult education to illustrate the costs and benefits of collaboration. Often, in neighborhoods that have several synagogues and a Jewish Community Center, I have noticed that each institution offers classes in introductory Hebrew. By collaborating, these institutions could provide beginning, intermediate, and advanced Hebrew language classes, offering more options to a broader audience without increasing their adult education budgets. There is still a cost to the collaborating institutions. Staff members have to agree on logistical issues, such as where classes are offered, how revenue is shared, and how each institution's role in the collaboration is publicized fairly. On the other hand, institutions also have an opportunity to market themselves and raise their community profile. And constituents benefit because they can now move seamlessly through different levels of Hebrew.

Younger generations have grown up clicking their way through cyberspace unencumbered by boundaries. They sometimes complain that many Jewish institutions create ideological barriers that inhibit participation. When younger adults see institutions making their boundaries more porous through collaboration, they may be more likely to participate in Jewish institutional life—another potential benefit of collaboration.

What is the single most important ingredient to successful collaborations? The answer is both simple and difficult: a trusting relationship between or among collaborating partners. No matter how much logical sense collaboration makes, if the parties involved do not approach the relationship with trust, respect, and commitment, it makes no sense for them to invest time and energy in collaboration. Without a foundation of trust, individuals who oppose the collaboration are likely to undermine it.

When each stakeholder in a collaboration wants the other(s) to be successful—and when this desire is expressed in word and deed—this helps build the trust that is essential. For example, when one synagogue in an adult-education collaboration celebrates a milestone, the other partners can be present for the celebration or write a note of congratulations. Small gestures like this can pay big dividends in goodwill that help collaborations work more smoothly. Additionally, collaborating groups must remember to communicate with one another frequently about the pieces of the collaboration for which each is responsible. When that communication doesn't happen, other members need to call attention to the problem and resolve it, instead of just feeling aggrieved.

Four Kinds of Collaboration

While collaborations can take various shapes, they generally fall into one of four categories.

The first type of collaboration is internal to an organization. In synagogues, as in any complex organization, departments can become compartments. People working on one aspect of synagogue life can be unaware of what is happening in another. As a result, some tasks are repeated unnecessarily, and even more important, opportunities to better serve the congregation as a whole are lost. For example, some congregations with preschools open spaces to nonmember families with the hope that these families will eventually become part of the congregation. If the preschool committee and the membership committee worked collaboratively and proactively to turn nonmember families into members, they could potentially increase congregational membership more than the membership committee could do alone, and the preschool could enjoy resources it could not access by itself. For example, the preschool and the membership committee could cosponsor a parenting series and share the costs of programming. The membership committee could also recruit older members who are adept at storytelling, and the preschool could use them as volunteers. By working collaboratively, the membership committee has a better chance of turning potential members into actual ones, and the preschool can enjoy more of the congregation's resources. Congregations often inadvertently overlook opportunities for internal collaboration. By practicing internal collaboration, synagogues can better utilize their resources and gain experience in collaboration that can help them develop partnerships outside their own organizations.

A second arena of collaboration is among Jewish organizations—between multiple synagogues or between synagogues and other Jewish organizations. Many synagogues now collaborate with one another with some regularity. As in the example about adult education earlier in the chapter, these partnerships have the potential to provide a better experience for participants. But there are many other possibilities for collaboration between synagogues and other Jewish organizations. Synagogues can partner with a local Jewish Family Service when offering premarital preparation classes or with a Jewish Community Center for a "Mommy and Me" program. In each of these examples, the synagogue can maintain and promote its individual identity while still partnering with another synagogue or organization.

The third area of collaboration, and this happens much less frequently, is partnership between synagogues and organizations outside the Jewish community.[1] What would happen if more synagogues developed partnerships with universities, hospitals, bookstores, department stores, supermarkets, and—of course—other communities of faith? With universities—everything from collaborating on Jewish studies programs to synagogues hiring a marketing intern from a university business program. With hospitals—creating a Jewish hospice program. With bookstores—a Jewish book festival. With department stores—a clothing drive for children. With supermarkets—a food drive that includes kosher food for a community food bank. With churches and mosques—a joint project for raising literacy levels in underperforming schools. Remember, most Jews spend the vast majority of their time outside the synagogue. By developing collaborations with organizations outside the Jewish community, synagogues can vastly extend their marketing and programming reach. These other organizations have their own e-mail and mailing lists and programming resources that complement those of synagogues.

Because of expulsions from many lands, Jews have historically been a geographically dispersed community. However, technologies today enable an exciting fourth dimension of collaboration. Jewish communities can overcome geographic barriers and reconnect with one another with great ease. They can collaborate on programs and initiatives, enrich their respective mutual communities, and strengthen the bonds of global Jewish peoplehood. Since synagogues exist in Jewish communities throughout the world, they can be the community common denominator. For example, with the help of technology, a Jewish community in Birmingham, Alabama, can create a social justice partnership with a community in the Ba'akah neighborhood of Jerusalem, and share strategies for combatting hunger and homelessness.

Additionally, many local federations already have partnerships with communities in Israel. Where feasible, congregations could build upon these connections to create shared-learning programs between children of the same age. For example, teenagers enjoy sharing music with one another, and learning about the favorite music of young people in another part of the world can foster cultural understanding. Following this same strategy, congregations can also create global partnerships with synagogues in other countries, an idea that opens wide the possibilities for building enriching relationships with Jews all over the world. Some communities in Israel and the United States are already exploring partnerships related to feeding the hungry and housing the homeless. In fact, because many Millennials already inhabit a global village, synagogues may find that involving Millennials in this aspect of synagogue life will attract and retain them as members.

Launching and Sustaining Collaborations

If your primary goal is to reduce costs immediately, collaboration is not the best strategy. Likewise, if you believe that your synagogue's greatest need is to conserve staff and volunteer time, you should consider other strategies. Over time, collaboration may indeed result in some savings of money and time, but those are byproducts of collaboration. And sometimes such savings aren't realized.

While saving resources is a legitimate institutional concern, collaboration is fundamentally about raising the quality of the experience for the individual participant or member. To achieve that goal, collaborations require

- a shared vision of stakeholder needs and desired outcomes;
- a commitment of human and financial resources;
- ongoing and honest communications; and
- a transparent process of working together.

None of these four requirements for successful collaboration occurs accidentally. Rather, they are realized when participants spend time discussing them and agreeing upon some guiding ground rules. For example, participants should discuss what measure they will use to determine whether the collaboration is successful. How will they communicate with one another? Will one member of the collaboration be designated as the group's communicator, or will all members be responsible for sharing information on a social media platform, like Google Docs or a wiki? Will participants make decisions by consensus or by majority vote? When funds are required, will stakeholders contribute the same amount of money, or pro-rata portions based on the size or budget of each organization? These are the kinds of questions that collaborating partners need to decide before they begin working together; otherwise, instead of accomplishing the work, they will spend time discussing the process for getting the work done. Successful collaborations respect the autonomy and uniqueness of each institution. Each institution must therefore be clear about its mission, its strengths and limitations, and its values, or it may find itself taking on roles for which it was unprepared.

Nonetheless, boundaries will remain fuzzy in even the best and most lasting collaborative relationships. There are several reasons this is true. In a new collaboration, the partners do not have past experience to guide them through the process and have not yet developed trusting relationships. In ongoing collaborations, changes in the internal needs of stakeholders may influence their roles in the collaboration, causing confusion among other participants. For example, a member who has been very active in the collaboration in prior years may need to reduce his or her role, because that person's congregation has eliminated a staff position, and remaining staff members must assume additional responsibilities. That internal organizational change causes this individual to request a diminished role in the collaboration. Unless she explains why she cannot shoulder a more active role, the other partners may feel her organization is no longer as interested in the collaboration. The behaviors of the collaborating partners are open to misinterpretation unless all are transparent about their individual needs and issues.

Collaboration involves letting go of some control. Therefore, those who hold power within an institution are sometimes reluctant to pursue collaboration wholeheartedly. This discomfort about relinquishing some power can manifest itself in several ways. For example, if adult-education committees from several synagogues and a Jewish Community Center are collaborating on an evening of Jewish learning, an adult-education chairperson from one congregation may try to ensure his organization holds a strong position. The other members of the collaboration must be willing to confront the problem and then all must work through a solution to make sure that all members have an equal voice. Or committee members may be working well on the collaboration, but the president of one congregation believes the effort is helping to showcase another congregation and resists cooperating, lest that other congregation recruit its own members. That congregation's representative in the collaboration must be willing to persuade the president to cooperate.

It is good practice to help individual stakeholders identify incentives for institutional power sharing. At the beginning of any collaboration, each party should clearly and honestly articulate why the partnership will make their organization stronger and why collaboration will help achieve the larger goals that their organization works for every day. Another way to overcome obstacles is to use a neutral third party to facilitate the collaboration, especially at the beginning of the process.

Strategies for Saving Resources

Although collaboration is not a primary strategy for conserving resources, nonprofit organizations can use a range of collaborative strategies to achieve efficiencies. My impression is that these strategies are better known in the wider world of nonprofits than in the synagogue community, so I introduce them here. I have drawn upon the work of David La Piana, a leading expert in nonprofit organizational structures such as collaborations and mergers, for an overview of the legal and structural implications of pursuing different types of relationships between nonprofit organizations, including synagogues.[2] Before entering into any of these relationships, synagogue leaders should understand their potential roles, responsibilities, risks, and benefits.

- *Management-services corporation:* A group of nonprofit organizations creates a separate entity for purchasing services and products, typically to increase administrative efficiencies and reduce costs. For example, several synagogues and other nonprofits might create a management-services corporation for shared IT, accounting, marketing, custodial, and catering services. Or they might do so to purchase health insurance for employees. There is no change to an organization's individual corporate structure in this arrangement, but by creating a separate corporation, individual synagogues and organizations can clearly follow how their resources are being spent and what the savings arc.
- *Joint-programming corporation:* This entity is similar to a management-services organization but is focused on programs instead of administrative services. A synagogue joins forces with another nonprofit to create a new organization to further specific programmatic ends, and the partner organizations share governance of the new organization. Again, participating organizations maintain their own corporate identities.
- *Strategic alliance:* In this arrangement, organizations that have shared interests and are similar in character, structure, and outlook work together for a process, project, or

issue. For example, a funder may require that two organizations work together in order to receive grant funding. These alliances tend to be deeper and longer lasting than the collaborations discussed earlier in the chapter, but, like collaborations, this arrangement enables each entity to retain its autonomy.

- *Merger:* Often known as the dreaded "M-word," a merger requires a change in corporate structures. A merger involves integrating all programmatic and administrative functions of multiple organizations with the hope of increasing administrative efficiency and program quality. Mergers occur when organizations with complementary or overlapping missions dissolve and create a new legal structure. As a part of this process, the new organization may create a new name, incorporate the names of the merged organizations, or use only one of the names. In this scenario, there is a "merger of equals." Another form of merger involves a smaller, more vulnerable organization merging with a stronger one. When this occurs, the surviving organization does not change its structure or name. While the organization that dissolves may refer to such an arrangement as a merger, it is really the equivalent of a takeover in the corporate world.

Synagogues typically have only two ways to resolve immediate financial problems—increase revenues and decrease costs—and these are often done simultaneously. But synagogues, like all nonprofits, have to consider the possibility that increasing revenues through higher program fees may price their services out of reach of potential audiences, while decreasing costs may diminish quality and leave supporters feeling shortchanged. Through collaborations and different partnership structures, synagogues can remain sensitive to costs while maintaining or even increasing quality experiences for members. The range of strategies described in this section can save synagogues resources while still enabling them to stay focused on quality. While I am generally skeptical about the idea of doing more with less, these strategies show that sometimes it is possible!

The Power of Networking

Nonprofit organizations can also work across different sectors with other organizations with the help of social media. For example, members of a congregation working on hunger issues can communicate with a congregation or organization in another state or even another country with great ease. Organizations located thousands of miles apart can now enter into long-term, voluntary relationships in order to share ideas, develop programs, and solve problems just as easily as they could if they were located just blocks from each other!

Networks are not new to the organizational scene. For example, Rotary clubs are comprised of individuals from the local business and professional community who meet to address social welfare issues. Social media platforms have turbocharged the creation and influence of networks, so club members from one location can now potentially meet with other members from any other chapter in the world.

Networks can present challenges to nonprofit organizations, because individuals who affiliate with a particular organization may also choose to engage in their own networking. These individuals may believe they speak for their synagogue or organization, even though they have not been officially empowered to do so. As a general rule, the more control synagogue leaders seek to maintain, the more likely they will feel threatened by networks. But if synagogues can loosen their grip, networks can be a source of enrichment. For example, a congregant who is passionate about Israel may maintain a Facebook group that attracts those in the community with similar feelings and may use this channel to let group members know about an upcoming program in the synagogue. This may cause more people who have similar feelings to attend the program. However, this same individual may be called by a local religion reporter who trolls the blogosphere for story ideas, and may make comments about Israel that do not reflect the "official" stance of the congregation or its rabbi.

Despite the risks, the rewards of encouraging staff members and volunteer leaders to network with others will bring the benefits of new ideas, new ways of approaching issues, and even new partnerships.[3] It may be difficult to quantify the value of networking, but it can take only one big idea to justify the cost of staff time that goes into creating meaningful networks.

Thinking Generously about Collaboration

When speaking about collaboration, I have persistently heard professional and volunteer leaders express two concerns:

- "If we collaborate, we might lose members to another synagogue." (Or, if the collaboration involves another Jewish nonprofit, the concern becomes, "They might donate to that organization or volunteer time for it.")
- "We are too ideologically different to work together."

After hearing these refrains for a couple of decades and watching synagogue involvement continue to decrease, I confess my impatience for such shortsighted concerns. My response to the first objection is, "Get over it, already!" If the number of people affiliated with the synagogues in your area is between 15 and 40 percent of the Jewish population, as it is in just about every significant Jewish population center in the United States,[4] who is your real competition—the synagogue nearest yours or other organizations and interests outside the Jewish community that have claimed the time of potential congregants?

With regard to ideology, we know that in many cases, ideology is not what drives synagogue involvement. More often, members focus on convenience, cost, educational quality, style of services, and the perceived warmth of the synagogue. While ideology may be a barrier at the staff level, it is rarely an insurmountable stumbling block for volunteer leaders. Synagogue staff and lay leaders can find many other areas that are ripe for collaboration even when defining ideological differences exist.

Leaders must think more broadly about how to reach people who have drifted from the synagogue and how to deepen the involvement of current members. Collaboration is one strategy for achieving these goals. Collaborations expand options for meeting new people and allow participants to enjoy new approaches to Jewish cultural, spiritual, educational, and intellectual pursuits. Collaborations enable staff members and volunteer leaders to acquire new perspectives on their work. While collaborations are not always easy, when done well, they can be rewarding to synagogue leaders and the communities they seek to serve.

When Collaboration Truly Conflicts with Religious Values

Having said this, I do not want to dismiss the possibility that collaboration can create a conflict in religious values. It's better to acknowledge when such unbridgeable differences exist and, instead, pursue collaborations with organizations where values are shared. Here are some illustrations of the difficulties that arise when a fundamental values divide exists between organizations.

Imagine the following situation: A group of federation lay leaders are preparing to gather for a daylong gathering at a local retreat center. The retreat center is not under kosher supervision but will accommodate the food choices of the federation. The federation has finally succeeded in recruiting a member of the Orthodox community to serve on its board. This board member explains that she will participate in the retreat only if the meals and snacks are provided by a kosher caterer under Orthodox supervision. Although a few other members of the board, including two non-Orthodox rabbis, keep kosher, their understanding of kashrut allows them to eat certain dairy foods that are not under rabbinical supervision. Board members know there's a substantial difference in cost between using an outside kosher caterer and using the onsite caterer. Given that the retreat is focused on how to best meet communal needs given ongoing decreases in the federation's annual budget, it is difficult to justify the additional cost. If you are the federation president, do you

- absorb the extra cost because of the federation's commitment to include all members of the community?
- provide kosher food only for that individual?
- forgo the retreat and instead schedule a four-hour evening meeting (with only kosher snacks) to avoid serving a meal?

Now, what happens if another member of your board hears about this issue and claims he is tired of always acceding to the requests of those who are more "religious"? He wonders, "How can this Orthodox board member be insensitive to the federation's desire to avoid additional costs so that more money can be used to serve the community. After all, kosher food can be made available for her—and two of the rabbis who are planning to attend have not raised the issue of kosher supervised food. So why is this an issue?"

If you work in the Jewish community today, you know how perplexing these kinds of issues can be. Let's name a few others for which resolutions may be even more elusive:

- The local Chabad rabbi has an attractive, experiential holiday program for children in religious school and wants to hold it at the Jewish Community Center (JCC). The local non-Orthodox rabbis warn the JCC director that if she hosts the program, they will urge their congregants to boycott the JCC, because the Chabad rabbi refuses to collaborate with them at community events and the JCC is a *community* space. As the JCC director, you know that only 50 percent of Jewish primary-school-aged children are in a synagogue religious school, and you believe it is important to try to reach the other 50 percent through programs like these. At the same time, you believe in the value of maintaining community harmony.

- The local board of rabbis, which includes rabbis from all denominations, appoints its president on a rotating basis, following the alphabetical order of the names of member congregations. The next presidential term is slotted for a rabbi who recently arrived in the community. This rabbi performs weddings between Jews and non-Jews, regardless of a couple's intention to raise the children as Jews. Several other rabbis will resign from the group if this new member is appointed as president. Your community has one of the very few rabbinical groups that still include broad denominational participation. If the group dissolves over this issue, it has a slim likelihood of reconvening.
- A Reform temple hosts a community program for the homeless, working in partnership with two neighboring churches. As Christmas approaches, the board of the temple votes to have a Christmas tree placed alongside the Chanukah menorah in the temple dining room. An Orthodox rabbi writes a letter in the local Jewish newspaper, blasting the congregation for violating Torah law on multiple levels. Is a response by other Jewish communal leaders warranted—and, if so, what should it be?
- Another flare-up of the "Who is a Jew?" issue occurs. The Conservative and Reform congregations band together to pressure the federation to withdraw funding from several

> overseas educational and social service programs that serve the secular Israeli public but are run under Orthodox auspices. If the federation does not withdraw funding, the congregations threaten to wage a public campaign against contributing to the federation.

The common denominator across these situations is the clash between liberal Judaism and Orthodoxy. During the past several decades, many of the flashpoints that used to arise among the established liberal denominations (Conservative, Reconstructionist, Reform) have diminished.[5] Two significant differences remain between the Conservative movement on the one hand and the Reconstructionist and Reform movements on the other. First, the Conservative movement requires a couple to obtain a Jewish writ of divorce, or *get,* to legally terminate a marriage. Conservatives also adhere to the tradition of determining Jewish legal status through matrilineal descent, namely that in addition to conversion into Judaism, Jewish status is conferred by virtue of a mother's Jewish origins and not a father's.

Fundamentally, however, the differences that arise among the various liberal movements are a matter of degree and not kind. Within a spectrum of belief, all agree that Torah and the subsequent tradition of rabbinic literature from which it sprang may be divinely inspired but is humanly created, with Jewish tradition taken seriously but not literally. Therefore, the process of consciously changing Jewish law, practice, customs, and values is perceived as advancing God's intentions.

The real fault lines are between Orthodoxy and the liberal movements. Although there is an incredible amount of ferment within the Orthodox community, one hallmark of any brand of Orthodoxy is belief in the Torah as the literal word of God delivered to Moses at Mount Sinai. Functionally, that belief means that concessions between tradition and modernity cannot be described as "compromise," because within that worldview, no individual has license to compromise the professed word of God. Even within modern Orthodoxy, which takes a more flexible approach toward rabbinically derived law as opposed to law based explicitly in the Torah, changes in Jewish law are more difficult to implement and, if they ever happen, come much later than in liberal communities.

As a result, non-Orthodox Jews sometimes perceive Orthodox Jews as antiquated in thinking and prejudiced against certain kinds of people. For example, so far with one exception, Orthodox rabbis who wish to retain their bona fides in the Orthodox community will not perform a wedding ceremony between two gay Jews. Non-Orthodox Jews who do not understand Orthodox belief may then level charges of bigotry against Orthodox Jews. Liberal Jews do not always understand the struggles Orthodox Jews have with these kinds of issues, nor do they recognize that Orthodox believers cannot resolve these questions in the same way liberal Jews can.

Conversely, some Orthodox Jews have too frequently labeled non-Orthodox Jewish practice as inauthentic and a distortion of "Torah-true" Judaism. Even worse, some more extreme segments of Orthodoxy actively seek to bar non-Orthodox Jews from living a full Jewish life in Israel and in the United States. They do not appreciate the reality that non-Orthodox expressions of Judaism have made Judaism and Jewish communities attractive to large swaths of people who would never consider Orthodoxy.

Let's just acknowledge that these groups often misunderstand one another, and each has at various times publicly claimed to be the "authentic" expression of Judaism, implying that other movements are illegitimate. The fault lines between Orthodox and liberal expressions of Jewish religious life are permanent, and dwelling on rifts that cannot be healed erodes the fabric of Jewish community. So how can those of us who are committed to collaboration handle situations where others with whom we might partner have some beliefs that offend our own reading of Judaism?

I am a firmly committed pluralist who has worked with every stripe of rabbi and denominational synagogue as well as those who identify themselves as independent. However, that does not mean I endorse collaboration at any cost. I have had to develop a list of personal values that help me navigate the tension that can arise between my cherished beliefs on specific issues and my commitment to collaboration. Here is my bottom line—a line I've drawn based on my experiences of some amazingly positive collaborations among diverse individuals as well as other attempted collaborations marked primarily by disappointment and frustration.

Where individuals show flexibility within their respective Jewish frameworks and strive to find ways to work with others who have different Jewish orientations, I am ready to struggle to collaborate, for their desire to collaborate validates those who are religiously different. But when people use demeaning and delegitimizing language or do not support good intentions for collaboration with action, I recognize that it will be more productive to look for other collaborative partners. I recommend that both individuals and organizations take the time to be clear about their parameters for collaboration. Doing so can prevent fruitless discussions and, alternatively, help expand the range of possible collaborations.

Personal Values for Reflection When Considering Collaborations

Successful collaborations ultimately require that collaborating partners are aligned in their core values. As in all relationships, when the parties agree about core values, they can overcome obstacles that naturally arise and create something greater together than they can alone. These are my core values in considering potential collaborations; what are yours?

- Love of the State of Israel—*ahavat medinat yisrael.* Create a central place in every Jewish organization for the State of Israel, which is a powerful generator of energy for Jews throughout the globe.
- Respect for all people—*k'vod ha-briot.* Honor the dignity, equality, and uniqueness of all people.

- Spirituality—*ruchaniyut.* Live in relationship with what came before us, what surrounds us, and what will come after us, with gratitude for the past and responsibility for the future.
- Love of the Jewish people—*ahavat yisrael.* Unconditionally accept people wherever they are in their Jewish development, remembering that Jewish development, a subcategory of human development, is an ongoing process.
- Defining people in—*keruv.* Strive to invite people into Jewish life, especially non-Jews who have Jewish family members, instead of drawing lines of exclusion.
- Respecting the diversity of the Jewish community—*shiv'im panim la-torah.* Embrace diversity in generations, family structure, racial background, and sexual orientation. These difference are a blessing. This diversity should be reflected in the leadership, programs, and processes of organizations.
- Humility—*tzneut lekhet.* Avoid the arrogance of proclaiming that one expression of Jewish life is the only correct way, and remain open to new expressions that may ultimately strengthen the Jewish future.
- Personal relationships—*panim-el-panim.* Seek to grow in our relationships with others, because when we deepen relationships, we grow individually and foster growth in others as well. A community rich in relationships is the wellspring of our creativity as a people.
- Contraction of self—*tzimtzum.* Know when to limit your presence so that others can step forward and flourish.
- Joyful living—*simcha shel mitzvah.* Celebrate the wonder of life and cultivate gratitude.
- Responsibility—*areyvut.* Commit to making the world a better place now and for future generations.
- Integrity—*shelaymut.* Be whole with yourself. You will increase chances of developing fruitful relationships—and you will be a happier person!

Chapter 4

Remixing the Rabbinate

Just as the synagogue rests on the precipice of essential change, the rabbinate is also undergoing a fundamental restructuring. This is happening now because of a convergence of technological and social changes that make individuals much less reliant upon rabbis and synagogues. As noted earlier, these changes include

- the unprecedented accessibility of Jewish learning, available in printed and digital formats, for purchase and often for free;
- an economic downturn that is pushing rabbinic compensation downward;
- competition from Jewish cultural experiences that lead people away from the synagogue;
- the impact of a substantial intermarried population that is at best ambivalent about synagogue involvement;
- the pervasive influence of Chabad, which does not charge membership dues like synagogues but instead relies upon voluntary contributions; and
- the coming-of-age of Gen Xers, with Millennials on their heels, who dislike the current model of most synagogues.

The cumulative effect of these and other changes is exponential and requires that rabbis, synagogue volunteer leaders, and seminary presidents must imagine what the rabbinate may soon look like. What follows is just one scenario that captures the profound transition the profession might undergo.

"Should I Enter the Rabbinate?"

The date was November 8, 2015, and it was Terri's thirty-fourth birthday. Terri and the rabbi of her congregation, Rabbi Bill, shared the same birthday, and she was looking forward to their annual birthday lunch together. She decided to tell him about her decision to apply to rabbinical school and ask for his "blessing" in the form of a recommendation.

Terri had been working for some time as an office manager in a midsize public relations firm. It was a good job that provided her with a stable income, and she took satisfaction in knowing she was helping the environment because her firm worked only with "green" clients. But for some time, she'd known she did not want to measure the value of her life by the number of clients her firm engaged and retained. Her application to rabbinical school was ready; she just needed Rabbi Bill's letter—and hopefully his encouragement as well.

When Terri raised the subject with Rabbi Bill, he was ambivalent. Of course, he would write her a recommendation and speak with the dean of the rabbinical school. But Rabbi Bill had long ago learned it was better to be honest than pleasantly agreeable, so he explained his ambivalence. On the one hand, Rabbi Bill still believed passionately in the work he did and experienced tremendous satisfaction from being able to support his congregants at pivotal moments in their lives. However, he could remember what his own rabbinate was like when he first began congregational work, and how it had changed after the financial crash of 2008, the subsequent prolonged recession, and the downsizing that affected many Jewish communal institutions.

The Great Recession negatively changed the economics of congregational life and accelerated trends—like decreasing membership retention and engagement and increasing competitive religious and cultural options to synagogues—that were already underway in the Jewish community. Prior to the near collapse of the economy, Rabbi Bill had earned a very comfortable living. However, he now earned about 35 percent less than he'd earned previously, and even that level of compensation was possible only because the congregation had sold its building and invested the income wisely and was now renting space. Although Bill still had had periodic financial worries, as time passed and he found that he was able to manage, his financial concerns had diminished.

As Bill reflected on these changes with Terri, he found himself thinking that while many of the abrupt changes he had experienced were punishing, some were actually satisfying. By working fewer hours per week for the congregation, he enjoyed his work more, because he and the board had made the difficult decisions about what rabbinic activities really mattered in the life of the community.

Tasks like teaching *b'nai mitzvah,* officiating at every life-cycle event, and leading services—activities he had previously viewed as essential parts of his rabbinate—were not as critical to the community as he had thought. Conversely, he was finding fulfillment in other elements of his work—helping the congregation envision the kind of community it wanted to be, teaching more intensively and frequently, providing spiritual direction for people in times of transition, and meeting with members of the congregation one-on-one or in small groups (something he'd always wanted to do but could never find time for).

Besides, he had found a new, unexpected outlet for a hobby that also fed his rabbinate. Bill had always loved to bake and realized he could earn some extra income by turning a passion into a financial proposition. He entered into a contract to use one of the kitchens at the Jewish-Christian Center—as the locals now referred to it, because "the J" had to partner financially with several churches in order to keep its building—to bake specialty cakes and challahs. While Bill did not advertise himself as a *mashgiach* (kosher supervisor), he used only kosher ingredients and his baking was superb, so he developed a clientele that liked the fact that a rabbi was doing the baking. Additionally, he realized that by using only organic products and by introducing a line of gluten-free products, he could attract an entirely different clientele.

After several months of baking, Bill realized that kids at "the J" were frequently stopping by the kitchen to spend time with him. Some of these kids were from his congregation, but many were not. Senior adults who were there for programming often came by as well. And he realized he was developing some wonderful relationships that he would otherwise never have had. Who would have thought he could develop a baking ministry!

Then, a local morning television show stopped by "Rabbi Bill's kitchen" and invited him to make a guest appearance as a rabbi-baker on her show. (Another rabbinic colleague of his had developed a second career by positioning herself as a religious-values cultural critic on a Sunday radio show.) Bill was such a hit when demonstrating how to braid challah that he signed a contract with the station to appear monthly on a segment called "Festing and Feasting," in which local clergy were invited to describe how their various culinary traditions expressed aspects of their respective major holiday celebrations. Rabbi Bill had to admit that he relished the experience and enjoyed meeting clergy from other religious faiths.

Bill's own rabbinate had changed dramatically over the past few years, and he was generally pleased with where the journey had led him. Still, he wondered to himself about how he should advise Terri. Given her limited knowledge of Hebrew and classical

Jewish texts, she was looking at six years of school, serious debt from student loans, and an uncertain job market. Not only would fewer jobs be available for her, but also the nature of rabbinic work would surely continue to shift.

For example, the previous year, the federation had stopped funding Israel and overseas needs. In contrast, although the local Jewish day school was fragile, a public elementary Hebrew charter school, modeled after the Spanish immersion school, was thriving. It had just expanded to grade three and had a substantial waiting list. Jewish and non-Jewish students there were not just speaking to one another in Hebrew; they were also working on projects with their peers in an Israeli classroom.

Another synagogue merger had just taken place. Still, within the past three years, two independent minyanim had been established. An aging Boomer population was interested in learning and spirituality, and with just about every major Jewish text now available in English and often for free, Rabbi Bill was teaching texts he'd not studied since rabbinical school. He enjoyed his work with the Boomer population immensely, and he realized the untapped influence this age group could have on the congregation and the general Jewish community.

Rabbi Bill was inspired by the work that many younger Jews were doing. They were leading so many changes in the general and the Jewish community! In the local healthy-food co-op, arts and culture, the environment, social justice—it was breathtaking to see how much activity was sponsored by Jews or in which there was a clear Jewish presence.

As Rabbi Bill prepared to answer Terri, he was unsure about how strongly he should recommend the path of the rabbinate to her, for her rabbinic journey would clearly be uncertain. The the Jewish community had downsized its institutions, although paradoxically, it had the capacity to upsize its reach and creativity. But what was the role of a rabbi amid all these changes? And what other changes were in store for the community? Would Terri find in the rabbinate the kind of personal career fulfillment she was seeking? What should he say to her?

The Rabbinate as Part-Time Avocation?

For much of Jewish history, the rabbinate was not a full-time profession. In fact, until the Middle Ages, it was against Jewish law for rabbis to receive payment for their services. The earliest reference we have to the rabbinate being a paid profession is from the end of the fourteenth century.[1] We know that some of the outstanding rabbis in Jewish history had other vocations. One of the most brilliant commentators on the Bible, Rashi (Rabbi Shlomo Yitzhaki) was a vintner. Maimonides (Rabbi Moshe ben Maimon), who left a prodigious legacy of philosophical and legal writings, was a physician to the royal court in Egypt. The rabbis and sages who appear in the rabbinic classics such as the Mishnah and Talmud held every imaginable job, from the most modest to the most sophisticated: Shammai was a builder,[2] Rabbi Oshaiyah made sandals,[3] Rav Yosef was a miller,[4] and Rav Huna raised cattle.[5] The modern rabbinate as we know it only emerged in the emancipation era and may prove to be an anomaly in Jewish history.[6]

It is helpful to view the transformation of the rabbinate within the general context of the restructuring of just about all industries and professions. For example, if you speak with a group of sixty-year-old medical doctors about the disruption of their practices with the introduction of health maintenance organizations (HMOs), you may gain some insight into the kinds of changes the rabbinate is experiencing. I vividly remember a conversation I had in 1985 with a doctor who was an active member of my congregation in Minneapolis. He spoke about how rapidly his practice was changing. Minnesota gave birth to HMOs, and the kinds of pressures doctors still often feel came to Minnesota early. This doctor was a caring and successful specialist, and while he earned a comfortable living, he worked hard and gave of himself to his patients and to the Jewish community. When I met him, he was in mid-career, and I imagine he still maintained a mental picture of what a long, successful practice of medicine looked like, an image based on the experiences of his teachers and mentors.

However, he shared that he was finding that he needed to devote significantly more time to insurance companies, having to balance his belief in high-quality care with the demands of insurance companies that increased his patient load. What was his financial reward? A decrease in compensation! While the current state of health care is still highly problematic and contentious, doctors have had to adjust their practices. Some of these changes are positive. For example, being more discriminating about tests and procedures, involving patients in achieving and maintaining good health, and developing patient outcomes are generally positive trends. Still, doctors face uncertain times and the health-care industry is anything but stable after several decades of change and reform.

This conversation has remained with me after all these years because it gives me context for understanding the restructuring of the rabbinate. Individuals can access educational, spiritual, and cultural resources on their own, independent of congregations. The Chabad movement continues to expand its network of synagogues, minyanim, religious schools, preschools, camps, and college campus houses, and undoubtedly is planning new initiatives. This movement abandoned the typical synagogue financial membership model of "joining" a synagogue for a relationship-based model of involvement. They understood that people who are emotionally connected to a rabbi and community are willing to contribute voluntarily. Chabad's global reach and its ability to work with families over a lifespan has been a disruptive force for many established synagogues. Similarly, Jewish cultural and social-justice organizations have siphoned interest in Jewish life away from synagogues, causing further instability in the congregational world.

Synagogues and all Jewish organizations must deal with the realities of demographic shifts. Although there is some dispute about the precise percentage, it is likely that the intermarriage rate during the past fifteen years has remained steady, at close to 50 percent.[7] Additionally, Jewish fertility rates are very low, and 20 percent of the Jewish population is elderly—a percentage that will continue to grow as the Jewish Boomer population ages.[8] When these Jews move to warmer climates, as they often do, they are not always interested in expensive synagogue memberships. Absent a serious investment in strategies to grow the Jewish people through outreach and conversion, demographics present an ominous challenge for synagogues.

We may well be approaching a time when the rabbinate does not offer as many full-time positions as it did in the past century. Even if the congregational rabbinate recovers some of its full-time positions, it seems unlikely we will see a return to the level of full-time employment that existed prior to the economic crash. The congregational and Jewish communal rabbinates are contracting, more because of social, technological, and demographic changes than economic ones. But even with this kind of future, and with awareness of the current structural and economic changes, the rabbinate can hold tremendous fulfillment for those who choose it, as it has throughout the ages.

I hope that the rabbinical seminaries, rabbinical organizations, and congregational organizations will jointly develop a strategy that takes into account these economic and cultural realities so that the highest caliber women and men will enter the rabbinate. Here are some of the questions that I hope a plan would address:

- Is expecting a five- to six-year rabbinical-school education at current tuition levels realistic? As an alternative, could instructional time focus on core requirements in Jewish

religious civilization, while also requiring continuing rabbinic education over several years, and, combined with mentoring, supply "practical rabbinics"? Another possibility might be to move the internships, mentorships, and pastoral and organizational curricular components into continuing rabbinic education.
- If stakeholders in rabbinical education would project the number of rabbis that the U.S. Jewish community is likely to need and find that there is a problem of overproduction, would they consider capping academic admissions?
- What are the essential services and roles for congregational rabbis?
- How can rabbinical organizations provide support to rabbis who are experiencing the dislocation of a rabbinate in transition?

Rabbinical education is like highway construction. By the time the work is completed, its capacity is often insufficient, or it does not solve the problems for long. The pace required for rabbinical curricular change does not match the typical institutional review processes generally in place. These issues require a new level of collaboration and creativity. Just as rabbis and congregants must rise to the challenge of collaboration, working together to create a shared, sustainable vision of a positive Jewish future, so must the triad of seminaries, rabbinical, and congregational organizations.

Evolution and Revolution of Rabbinic Roles

I hope that some combination of seminaries, rabbinical organizations, and congregational associations will begin to act in a coordinated fashion to lead the effort for change in both rabbinical education and the rabbinate itself—and that they will do so immediately. In the absence of such a coordinated effort, I would suggest that individual rabbis and enlightened congregations take the initiative and prepare for impending changes. As a friend of mine once said, "Some people make change happen. Other people say, 'What happened?'" If you are a rabbi, in which group of people do you want to place yourself?

Today, congregational rabbis are expected to be programmers, teachers, pastoral counselors, community-relations representatives, fund-raisers, ritual guides, administrators, and slightly holy but still accessible individuals with a good sense of humor. They work extremely hard, but many of them are caught in a structure that underutilizes their strengths and plays to their weaknesses. Many rabbis spend much time at board and committee meetings. It's no surprise to me that many of them say they would be much more fulfilled if they spent less time in meetings and more time teaching and doing outreach.

As we move further into the twenty-first century, some rabbinic roles will remain essential, but will be expressed differently—the most obvious one being rabbi as teacher. Other roles will need different degrees of emphasis—some more, some less. Still other roles will be new, while some former roles may disappear altogether. I will examine each of these, focusing first on those roles that are likely to remain constant, then exploring roles that require reframing, and then looking at new functions that rabbis will need to perform. I will conclude the chapter with a discussion on the merits and drawbacks of the rabbi also functioning as chief executive officer of the congregation (or, more accurately, chief professional officer) and, in a related vein, current rabbinic roles that can be deemphasized.

Roles That Remain Essential

While we are living at a time when there is more discontinuity than continuity with the past, some historic rabbinic roles should not change. Every generation of rabbis is charged with the primary responsibility of leading the Jewish people. In support of that essential role, rabbis must mobilize people to help them fulfill and enrich their leadership potential and must also share in the responsibility of helping to secure funds for community needs.

The Rabbi as Dreamer and Visionary Leader

It saddens me how many Jews, the people who brought the teaching of progressive ethical monotheism to the world, are now so ambivalent or negative about the Jewish religion. Nation-wide internal surveys of the Jewish community[9] and external surveys and analyses about religious attitudes of Americans from researchers like Robert Putnam and David Campell[10] regularly find that U.S. Jews connect very little with the religious or spiritual aspects of Judaism. The majority of American Jews self-identify as cultural or secular and, as a group, exhibit less involvement with their religious institutions than any other religious group.[11]

The Bible, Judaism's foundational text, is replete with spiritually audacious individuals. We also find words like "vision" (*hazon*) and "dream" (*halom*) peppered throughout the Scriptures. What makes biblical narratives so compelling is the willingness of our ancestors to strive to fulfill a dream and inspire a community of like-minded dreamers along with them.

We see these same willing spiritual virtuosos throughout Jewish history, continuing into our own era.[12] Each historical period has produced spiritual dreamers and visionaries, rabbis who have changed the communities of their time and bequeathed a legacy to the following generations.[13] As rabbis are the exemplars of the best of Jewish religiosity and spirituality, they have to assume significant responsibility for improving the perception of the Jewish religion among U.S. Jews. Fortunately, the contemporary American Jewish community has some outstanding rabbis, like the rabbis who are featured in chapter 5. They inspire members of the Jewish community as well as those in other faith communities with their dreams of a more compassionate, just, and ethical world. I believe there are many more who could do likewise, but they have yet to find a more public voice.

So I am making a plea to my colleagues: Enlarge your vision of what Judaism can contribute to individuals and the world so that you will change the perception of many Jews that Judaism is irrelevant. You know that many people in your community are spiritually hungry. Indeed, a recent study by JumpStart, a Jewish nonprofit dedicated to strengthening emerging, innovative organizations, indicated that 54 percent of Jewish "start-up" organizations focus on spirituality and ritual. This finding confirms yet again the need for more vision-driven Jewish spiritual pathways than many synagogues currently offer.[14] Those rabbis who can offer a compelling alternative vision of the world are the ones who will find an audience in the twenty-first century—and we need more of them today.

The Rabbi as Talent Scout

One of the most fulfilling jobs a rabbi has is to be a talent scout for the congregation. Rabbis have an incredible opportunity to help people grow Jewishly through engaging them in volunteer activities for the congregation. When more individuals experience growth as Jews, the community also grows. As a general rule, congregations can become significantly better at tapping into the vast expertise in their congregational membership. As noted in chapter 2, given the generally high levels of education and professional accomplishment of many congregants, volunteers remain an underutilized source of tremendous expertise for congregations.

Volunteers are a great source of specific expertise that congregations and other nonprofits could not otherwise afford. Marketing, website maintenance, program innovation, fund development, visitation of grieving or sick members, community interfaith work—the ways in which volunteers can share their expertise with a congregation or spiritual community are vast. In an age of diminished financial resources, volunteers are more valuable than ever, and when you tap into their passions, they will often exceed expectations.

Often, it seems that rabbis underestimate the importance of investing time in identifying talents and developing new volunteers. They return to the same volunteers because they have not done the planning that would enable them to think more carefully about who might be involved in an endeavor. This weakness puts rabbis in good company, for the great biblical leader Moses often seemed to forget he had a talented community at his disposal. He must have known it in theory, because when God and Moses' father-in-law, Jethro, reminded Moses that he had people to help him meet the insatiable demands of his congregation, he listened (Exod. 18:13–24). But the daily demands of his work apparently made him forget it in practice. The lone leader will soon burn out, while the leader who understands how to unleash the talent of volunteers will create a truly awesome enterprise.

The Rabbi as Fund-raiser

If you are a rabbi and you do not feel some satisfaction from fund-raising, you are likely headed for trouble. Now is the time to face those aspects of fund-raising that evoke discomfort for you. In a market era when many people are experiencing shrinking resources, knowing how to be a part of a team effort to solicit financial contributions is an essential part of the rabbinate. Indeed, it can be exceptionally gratifying to help someone of significant financial means be a partner in strengthening Jewish life; to watch a layperson catch fire with enthusiasm when you become the catalyst for bringing to the surface an idea that a donor has about improving Jewish life.

Given the economic pressures synagogues face, rabbis must be involved in fund-raising. Generally, they should meet with potential donors along with a team of volunteer leaders and not alone. When volunteers explicitly solicit gifts from donors, rabbis then preserve their roles as visionary leaders in these conversations.

Roles Needing Reframing

What does it mean for rabbis to "reframe" roles that congregants have always expected them to fulfill? It means that rabbis must learn to think and act differently when it comes to these traditional responsibilities. In other words, reframing involves a conceptual dimension and an action component.

For example, rabbis have always needed to connect regularly with congregants. In an era when social media tools like blogging, Facebook, and YouTube have created a vast number of new ways to remain connected, how should a rabbi think about what it means to develop relationships with congregants? How frequently should a rabbi update his or her Facebook page? What happens when a "nudnik" congregant e-mails a rabbi several times each week, expecting the rabbi to respond to every e-mail?

By first thinking broadly about a particular role, rabbis can then act in a more strategic manner. That's what reframing means—conceptually rethinking an existing role and then acting in new or modified ways.

The Rabbi as Passionate Leader

Few courses in rabbinical school or continuing education programs are designed to help rabbis think about communicating with passion in their rabbinate. Passion is that quality that evokes excitement, curiosity, and inspiration in others and mobilizes them to try to accomplish a goal. Those rabbis with passion will be the ones who will thrive in their rabbinates in this still young century. Why? While abundant information about Judaism is easily accessible, information does not replace the desire for a living relationship with a great teacher and a powerful exemplar of Jewish life, indications of a passionate rabbinate.

People often confuse passion with charisma. As charisma is used colloquially, it relates more to performance and showmanship. It is not the same as passion. What are some of the differences between passion and charisma?

- Passion is centered on a dream; charisma is anchored in the self.
- Passion inspires others to work together; charisma can create divisions.
- Passion is about purpose; charisma is about drama.
- Passion exists comfortably with humility; charisma is in conflict with it.
- Passion endures and lifts people around it; charisma often creates a crash-and-burn syndrome and takes others down with it.
- Passion helps to build community because those feeling it respond to a higher calling; charisma, however, diminishes community because people ultimately perceive that the ego behind the charismatic leader leaves little room for others.

Passion is a good thing for rabbis, but charisma can be dangerous and destructive. Passion is about uncovering core issues and drawing from that knowledge an authentic sense of purpose. It means finding one's voice and then not losing it over the years.

Many rabbis begin their service with a sense of calling for a transcendent purpose—this is the passion that brought most of them into the rabbinate. But the distractions of congregational politics and the countless lengthy discussions over small issues can mute that sense of higher purpose. The result is that rabbis become less inspiring, because they've learned to play it safe rather than to speak from their authentic selves. That's when rabbis become dull. They may be able to fake charisma, but they can't pretend to have passion. Rabbis can learn techniques for giving a good sermon, teaching an exciting class, or offering a stirring eulogy, but we need rabbis who are more than technicians. We need rabbis who maintain their passion for the challenges of a calling that is increasingly complex. And we need congregations who will support and reward rabbis for doing so.

The Torah warns of the dangers of charismatic leaders as well as the differences between them and leaders who were not only charismatic but also passionate. The biblical Korach was charismatic and caused a catastrophe (Num. 16:1–35). On the other hand, Moshe Rabeinu, Moses, was the rabbi par excellence. The trait that characterizes his leadership more than any other is humility—a humility that repeatedly averted disaster. Charisma, over time, seems to defeat humility, often creating out-of-control situations. Conversely, the compatible qualities of humility and passion have the power to create enduring dreams.[15]

The Rabbi as Educator

Few educators spend a routine day teaching a group of preschoolers in the morning, older adults at lunchtime, middle-school children in the late afternoon, and middle-aged adults in the evening. Yet that is not an unusual schedule for a congregational rabbi. And in recent years, the audiences for adult and family education have increased. Given the heavy expectations on rabbis as educators, more attention needs to be paid to helping rabbis excel in this role.

I have witnessed too many painful scenarios where a rabbi's lack of educational theory was evident. One morning I watched a rabbi interact with preschool children using vocabulary suited for a college-preparatory examination. These preschoolers were pleasantly behaved—but completely inattentive to what the rabbi had to say. Later that week, I witnessed another colleague speak to educated adults as if they were children. I would be willing to wager that the class was cancelled because they felt disrespected.

A colleague of mine shared another true story that illustrates the need for rabbis to acquire a working knowledge of effective teaching for people at varying stages of human development. This colleague once invited his father-in-law to a lecture that he was giving at a local Jewish Community Center. After the lecture, the son-in-law inquired what his father-in-law thought about the lecture. His father-in-law praised him by saying it was one of the best lectures he had heard recently. The son-in-law was, of course, flattered and curious. He asked, "Dad, what made it such a good lecture?" To which his father-in-law responded, "I told you, I could actually hear you!" Just a little bit of knowledge about how older adults learn could make their experience so much more enjoyable.

At this moment in history, four different generations of people are alive, from newborns to 100-plus-year-olds. Each generation has specific emotional, spiritual, cognitive, and physiological developmental needs. Rabbis do not need to be experts in all of these stages. However, rabbis need to be aware of the fundamental arcs of development so that they can prepare and present with their audiences in mind. Many rabbis who are already average or slightly above-average educators could achieve excellence with just a little training and mentoring.

In view of the impact of technology on education, it is essential that rabbis also learn how to exploit technology to enhance their teaching. I read a story in the business magazine *Fast Company* that drove this point home. Actually, it wasn't the story that shook me to the core, but the pictures. Why? One picture was of three-year-old twins holding iPhones. The reporter then described how they were using apps to learn how to spell, read, and learn songs. She then noted:

> [These twins] . . . belong to a generation that has never known a world without ubiquitous handheld and networked technology. American children now spend 7.5 hours a day absorbing and creating media—as much time as they spend in school. Even more remarkably, they multitask across screens to cram 11 hours of content into those 7.5 hours. More and more of these activities are happening on smartphones equipped with audio, video, SMS, and hundreds of thousands of apps.[16]

The implications of this reality for rabbis and, indeed, all Jewish educators are staggering. Roll forward less than a decade to a time when the children of this generation will become bar and bat mitzvah. Will rabbis be ready to work with a generation of self-directed learners? As rabbis work with the first and second waves of young adults who have grown up in a technology-saturated environment, are rabbis ready to rethink their roles as educators, seeing themselves less as "source of knowledge" and more as "guides to knowledge and embodiment of Jewish life now"?[17] Rabbis will need to quickly learn how to wisely incorporate technology into their teaching role if they are to remain relevant educators.

Another challenge for rabbis in achieving excellence as teachers is to be aware of communicating in a multimedia environment. Public speaking, using evolving social media for education, appearing on cable television and radio—each medium requires basic training if it is to be used effectively. Most often, rabbis who are educated at accredited seminaries know a significant amount of Torah. However, it often remains locked inside them, because they do not know how to communicate in a way that resonates with their audience. In one passage in the Talmud, the following question is asked: "To what is a scholar to be compared? To a vial of fragrant ointment. When its cover is removed, the fragrance of its ointment is diffused. When it is covered, its fragrance is concealed."[18] Communications skills can help release the fragrance of Jewish wisdom into an atmosphere that is often filled with noxious values. Rabbis have a unique and unprecedented opportunity to shape Jewish lives and their broader communities. They can be successful by taking the time to learn about human development, educational theory, technology, and communications. And given the teaching expectations that congregants have of rabbis, it is an exceptionally worthwhile investment of their time!

The Rabbi as Cultural Mediator

In the words of the psalmist, rabbis are privileged to work "in the courts of the Lord," often all day, every day (Ps. 116:19). In many cases, rabbis work with a dedicated team of staff and volunteers who spend most or a significant part of their lives around the synagogue as well. They also interact with the "regulars," those who come for Shabbat and holy day worship, and those who can be counted upon to be there for almost any program. These are the people who anchor their lives around synagogues and are grateful for the meaning it provides. For them, the synagogue is generally working well.

However, these individuals are the minority. Ask yourself: How much time does the average, non-Orthodox, American Jew who pays synagogue dues actually spend in the synagogue in most years? Here is my generous estimate:

- eight hours for Rosh ha-Shanah and Yom Kippur;
- six hours at other Shabbat and holy day services;
- seven hours for life-cycle events of family or friends; and
- four hours for special programs.

If these estimates are even close, that means the average American Jew will spend only twenty-five hours, little more than a day per year, in the synagogue—and most of that time is spent passively, that is, observing others' actions and listening to their words. When I have asked colleagues around the country how many hours they believe the average non-Orthodox Jew spends in the synagogue each year, they usually report even less time, somewhere between twelve and fifteen hours. Thus, while synagogue involvement is central to the lives of a narrow percentage of individuals, the vast majority of American Jews, including many who pay membership dues, have decided the synagogue does not speak their language. That means the synagogue has to take on the role of cultural mediator, helping to connect timeless Jewish values, practices, and beliefs with current events in the outside world, where the majority of Jews spend most of their time.[19]

Being a cultural mediator does not mean latching on to the latest trendy fashion. Rather, it means addressing people's real, everyday concerns about health, relationships, work, play, spiritual and intellectual growth, children, money, and loss—the stuff of daily life. While remaining true to the tradition as the rabbi understands it, each synagogue must address these subjects and help individuals experience the value of exploring them in a community. It means recrafting the interpretation of core Jewish values and practices to resonate with contemporary sensibilities.

Certain rabbis already do this, and we will meet some of them in the next chapter. Their sermon topics, teaching, bulletin articles, and social-action projects address issues that matter to people. But this kind of cultural mediation has to be done more systematically and more frequently. If it were happening more often, we might see greater numbers of people being shaped by the synagogue and valuing a synagogue community.

The Rabbi as Entrepreneur

Why must rabbis think of themselves as entrepreneurs? There is a saying that goes, "If you do what you've always done, you'll get what you've always gotten." And we know that "what we've always gotten" is unacceptable today. Too many Jews find Judaism irrelevant to their lives. If we continue "doing what we've always done," we will miss the great potential we have as a community to extend a hand to the increasing numbers of spiritual seekers who are not Jewish yet want to explore Judaism.

Entrepreneurs are people who see opportunities that don't yet exist, or who see a problem as a chance to act on a better idea. They take risks. They make some mistakes—but they can have great successes, because they do not settle for a status quo that is often just adequate. They don't just adapt to their environment. They try to create the environment they want. The attributes and attitudes of rabbinic entrepreneurs are no different from those of business entrepreneurs. It's just that the rabbi's domain is the synagogue or some other Jewish entity instead of a business.

Nonetheless, there is an inherent tension between the more normative role of rabbi as standard-bearer of tradition and the relatively new role of rabbi as entrepreneur. Business entrepreneurs are not bound by the past. In fact, they usually want to be liberated from it! In contrast, regardless of denomination or religious orientation, faith-based leaders are in the business of legacy and tradition. They are tasked with transmitting the traditions of their heritage, denomination, and institution, as well as adapting these traditions so the community can maintain integrity with the past as they understand it. "Religious entrepreneurship" is not quite a contradiction, but the entrepreneurial spirit and the religious spirit do not coexist easily. And it is important to acknowledge that fact so that rabbis can understand the discomfort they may feel in turning up the dial on their entrepreneurial skills.

Evangelical Christians and some corners of the more fundamentalist Jewish community seem to know how to maintain equilibrium between traditional practice and entrepreneurial approaches to that practice. These groups have co-opted the zeitgeist of our times, and appeal to people's need for autonomy that enables them to feel safe enough to become a part of a community. Just watch a Rosh ha-Shanah or Passover video by Aish HaTorah,[20] an Orthodox educational and outreach organization. Yes, you can debate whether these more fundamentalist expressions of Judaism haven't themselves been co-opted by modernity and sacrificed some of their own spiritual integrity, but they at least offer laboratories for learning about the results of entrepreneurial practices.

Specifically, if you wanted to cultivate a more innovative disposition, how would you go about it?

- Practice saying yes to possibilities and opportunities.[21] Once you are certain about your religious boundaries and what you can't or won't do, think about what you *can* do. I cannot emphasize this piece of advice enough.
- Meet with people who have had success with start-ups in the for-profit and nonprofit worlds.
- Learn the basic principles of entrepreneurship from successful businesspeople.
- Learn from competitors, like independent minyanim and Chabad.
- Subscribe to blogs, newsletters, or podcasts related to innovation in science, technology, arts, entertainment, marketing, and education.
- Talk regularly with people in different age demographics. Learn what interests and concerns them.

Every generation has had its rabbinic entrepreneurs. Sometimes, historical calamities have imposed the need for creative responses to devastation. In other ages, when relations between Jews and non-Jews were decent, rabbinic entrepreneurs expressed their creativity by incorporating aspects of their broader culture into the Jewish tradition. Still, if you are not wired to take risks and see opportunities others don't, cultivating an entrepreneurial spirit is challenging. But it is possible, as the rabbis featured in the next chapter have shown. And even if it is difficult for a rabbi to take the lead as a religious entrepreneur, every rabbi has people in his or her congregation who will be willing to bring some innovation to synagogue if asked.

Reducing Some Current Rabbinic Roles

Although rabbis need to shift into new roles and deepen existing ones, some aspects of their work need to be minimized or discarded. Here are some for consideration:

- *Pastoral counseling.* While rabbis will always have an important role in pastoral counseling, this is one area they can scale back. Rabbis can partner with more Jewish Family Service counseling staff or develop a "train-the-trainer" approach, and train Jewish mental health professionals to provide a Jewish spiritual dimension to their counseling.
- *Attending meetings.* Memo to board and committee members: Even if you would like to have your rabbi at a meeting, how critical is his or her attendance—really? Memo to rabbis: Your board and committees can manage without you if you (1) meet with the chair or cochairs and agree upon project or issue parameters and outcomes, and then (2) have periodic check-ins with them as a project or process develops.
- *Officiating at life-cycle rituals.* If you allow the parents of a bat mitzvah to address their daughter during services, does the rabbi have to give another charge to the child? What other life-cycle events could friends and family lead without a rabbinic presence?

I have great empathy for the unrealistic demands facing rabbis and other members of the clergy. Anyone who has worked as a congregational rabbi (or even worked with rabbis) knows that the gap between what one rabbi can do and what many congregants expect is one that can never be bridged. It is a tension that rabbis learn to live with over time. But rabbis and lay leaders do have the power to initiate discussions with other volunteer leaders about how the rabbi's time can be used in ways that most benefit congregants. In these tumultuous times for congregations, such conversations are essential.

In a related vein, a perennial organizational issue for synagogues is whether the rabbi should function as the chief executive or professional officer. In very small congregations, where the rabbi is the only full-time professional staff person or there is a rabbi and a full-time educator, the rabbi is a de facto chief professional officer! But, many congregations, from small to large, have an executive director. Where does the proverbial buck stop—at the rabbi's desk or at the executive director's desk? Remember that regardless of the issue, the rabbi is often called upon to resolve it. If the issue is about administration and the rabbi acts, the executive director may feel challenged. But if the executive director acts in a way that the rabbi believes does not honor Jewish values, the rabbi may feel like his or her rabbinic authority has been ignored. Is there a right answer to this question?

A rabbi has to fulfill some roles of a CEO but not all of them. He or she should strive to infuse all aspects of the synagogue with Jewish values and practices. Lay leaders may distinguish between the religious and the business dimensions of a synagogue, but synagogue budgets and business practices also make a statement about Jewish values, so finances require rabbinic input as well. Other reasons to include rabbis in the "business" aspects of synagogue life include the fact that a rabbi is one of only a handful of people who look at the congregation holistically. He or she may also have access to information that other key decision makers do not.

For all these reasons, rabbis will help themselves and their congregations by acquiring essential knowledge about managing and leading nonprofit organizations. Prayer, education, social-action projects, and other programs do not run well when effective administrative systems are not in place. If the synagogue is perceived as lacking in fiscal controls, donors will be skeptical about contributing to the congregation. But what a congregation really needs is for the rabbi to have a true partner on the finance and operations side, so that the rabbi can focus on the tasks of leadership, vision, teaching, and the like. Rabbis are vital to these areas of Jewish life, and the more time they can devote to them, the better off the synagogue will be.

The profile of an executive director who could form an ideal partnership with a rabbi would include someone who has a solid business background in the for-profit or nonprofit world, has studied in Jewish day school or attended Jewish camps as a youth, lives a Jewish life, has background or training in Jewish studies, and understands that all decisions in the synagogue should be considered in the light of Jewish practice and tradition. Such individuals are very difficult to find, but synagogues can provide continuing education funds for executive directors so that over time they can fill in their experiential and educational gaps.

Sometimes less is more. The less time rabbis devote to operational and administrative aspects of synagogue life, the more time the rabbi has to perform essential rabbinic functions. In an environment of tight resources, organizations that focus staff members' attention in their area of expertise have a better chance of surviving. In the end, there is no such abstraction as "an organization." An organization is only as good as the people who constitute it. Therefore, it is critical not only to have the right people on board but also to make sure they are using their time to maximum benefit.

The Twenty-First-Century Rabbi

The rabbinate as we have known it since its emergence in the latter half of the nineteenth century is undergoing rapid structural change. Existing roles need to be reconsidered, and new roles need to be adopted—now, for today's rabbinate. The roles of dreamer and visionary leader, passionate leader, talent scout, educator, cultural mediator, fund-raiser, and entrepreneur are likely to be essential aspects of rabbinic work in the decades ahead.

Other professionals in the nonprofit and even for-profit sectors share some of these roles. However, whether the role is old or new, it is the incorporation of Torah in its broadest meaning that imbues each role with rabbinic authenticity. Rabbis become influential leaders when they anchor each function in textual, theological, historical, and ethical perspectives. That reality increases the urgency for rabbis and volunteer leaders to seriously examine what constitutes essential and value-added rabbinic work and to make changes accordingly in how rabbis invest their time and energy.

Chapter 5

Pathways to Synagogues of the Future

The scenario of the fictional Temple Torah (chapter 2) as well as the ideas about how the role of the rabbi might be reimagined (chapter 4) were designed to stimulate your creative thinking about what a truly reenvisioned synagogue and rabbinate could look like. Your reactions to those chapters may have run the gamut of feelings, ranging from optimism to skepticism, from curiosity to disbelief. But even if you still have doubts about whether a synagogue like Temple Torah could or even should exist, we hope you will find this chapter especially useful. In it, you will hear the voices of ten rabbis who are grappling with many of the same questions the scenario raises and pioneering new ways of reenvisioning the mission and structure of their congregations.[1]

If you are primed to begin experimenting with radical innovation—"radical" in the sense of the word's Latin origins, which suggest getting at the *root*—then these rabbis will inspire you with examples of what is possible. But even if you are unsure about the wisdom or possibility of such fundamental change, we hope these voices will encourage you to consider how—in the words of Rabbi Abraham Joshua Heschel—you might take an innovative "leap of action" in your own congregation.

That being said, these interviews are not meant to prescribe what rabbis should do in their congregations, nor are they intended to directly support my own conclusions in other parts of the book. Rather, in the spirit of an exploratory analysis, I hope these rabbis' reflections will expand the discussion beyond my own thinking and offer new ways of responding to the rapidly changing conditions of the prevailing American synagogue model.

Our team interviewed ten rabbis, spending approximately one hour in each interview.[2] We selected these rabbis based on their reputations among their peers, their congregations' perceived commitment to innovation, and recommendations from others in our networks. We spoke with rabbis who were trained by Conservative, Orthodox, Reform, and Reconstructionist seminaries so that we could explore whether their responses differed by denomination. Our goal was not to launch a scientific study but to identify rabbinic change agents and engage them in conversations about their work. We did not spend time in each congregation to observe the degree to which the ideas about innovation were actually implemented. Although the findings from our interview process do not carry the reliability and validity accepted among social scientists, they are rich in insights, experiences, and responses to the complexities of congregational life today. Additionally, these findings suggest intriguing areas of future inquiry into rabbinic leadership.

We asked our subjects the following questions:

- Generally speaking, what makes your synagogue different from others?
- What aspects of your congregation do people seem to find most appealing?
- What's the big idea that lies at the core of your mission?

- In developing your mission and vision, where do you look for lay leadership?
- What role do you play, and what role do laypeople play?
- Where does the thrust of your leadership come from—you, your volunteer leaders, or some combination?
- How do the programs and activities you offer bring your mission to life?
- Beyond decisions about ritual, what role does your theology play in the work you do?
- What individuals or institutions have been inspirations for you in your work?
- How have you navigated the problems associated with the traditional membership model that has characterized relationships between individuals and congregations? Do you have any plans to redefine this relationship?
- How do you involve volunteers? Have you changed or modified the traditional board and committee structure? If so, how have congregants reacted to these changes?
- What is the role of the rabbi in your synagogue? Does your role differ from how you understand a traditional rabbinic role? If so, how?
- How would you describe your congregation's relationship with its denomination?
- What role does technology play in helping your congregation fulfill its mission?

These questions were designed to explore the connections between rabbinic theology, congregational mission, and organizational structure. In other words, how does a rabbi's personal theology become manifest in the congregational mission, and how is that mission expressed through the structures that congregations create and use to pursue their mission? We have categorized interview findings by topic and not by person. We decided to go in this direction for a few reasons. First, we want you to focus not on who said it but what was said. When individual rabbis have been profiled in prior works, we have heard other colleagues respond with frustration about how they could never "be like Rabbi X." But, as we will contend later, true leadership is not merely a function of personality. Leadership is a quality that can be cultivated. Beyond that, we believe it is much healthier to focus on questions of mission, theology, and structure, because everyone can learn something in these areas that can benefit their rabbinate.

What We Learned

The rabbis we interviewed offered rich and nuanced perspectives on their own professional journeys, but a number of key themes emerged that transcended denomination and geographic location.

The Vision Thing

Author Lewis Carroll once said, "If you don't know where you're going, any road will take you there." Although we did not explicitly ask the rabbis we interviewed if they were familiar with this quote, it is clear that each of them is guided by a strong sense of purpose and mission. All of these rabbis have a vision of Judaism's role in the world and their congregation's piece in helping to actualize it. And while their own rabbinic visions are clearly evolving, they remain faithful to their core purpose.

Their visions are big in two respects. First, they are large enough to encompass an individual member's personal search for meaning within a communal and global vision. It was a given for these rabbis that their congregants were on an ongoing Jewish journey, but their consistent message was the personal journey must ultimately be placed within the context of the broader congregational mission. Rabbis were concerned that without ongoing reminders of the purpose and work of the congregation, individual searches for personal meaning would slip into narcissism.

The vision of these rabbis is large in an additional sense, as well. We describe this dimension of their vision as "transcendent." By *transcendent,* we mean that these rabbis create a context for congregants in which the performance of ritual, study, and social good are not particularistic, isolated ends in and of themselves. Rather, they are mutually reinforcing stepping-stones toward fulfilling the broader vision. Even in our brief interviews with these rabbis, we were inspired by their compelling dreams regarding Judaism's impact on the broader world. We can easily imagine that their congregants feel the same way, especially because they hear their rabbis' words regularly and are able to watch them turn ideas into actions.

Spiritual Confidence

Another theme that echoed across these interviews was that of spiritual confidence. These rabbis believe deeply in the approaches to Jewish life they have developed for themselves, their congregations, and their congregations' role in the world. For many of them, Judaism serves as the foundation for their critique of social and economic problems in the broader world. For others, Judaism is the source for ultimate personal and communal meaning. Regardless of their essential beliefs, these rabbis are confident that Judaism has an invaluable contribution to make to individuals, communities, and the world. They do not adopt a triumphalist or exclusive attitude, suggesting that their way was the only "correct" way. Instead, their shared attitude can be summarized as, "I believe Judaism offers a truly valuable approach to life, and I have the spiritual confidence to proudly and publicly bring my approach to my community and the broader world."

All the rabbis we interviewed are indeed lovely individuals. But it was clear to us that their ultimate goal in congregational work is not to be universally lauded and liked. They have taken public stands on issues of importance to them and, as anyone in public life knows, taking a stand on any issue will attract some people and alienate others. We assume all these rabbis have their detractors and their supporters. But our impression is that their spiritual confidence in their beliefs enables them to care more about a consistent stand on their core principles and less about public opinion polls and favorability ratings.

Rabbis with Rebbes

In working with rabbis throughout the years, I have observed that there are two kinds of rabbis: those who have rebbes and those who just have colleagues they call upon for advice. What is the difference? A rebbe is someone who helps mold the character and worldview of another rabbi. He or she doesn't merely provide answers to specific questions but offers an approach to understanding and applying Judaism in its totality to contemporary life. As Mishnah Avot 1:1 suggests, a rebbe transmits a living body of Torah to a disciple.

When we asked these rabbis who had influenced them, almost all of them readily spoke about a contemporary rabbinic influence, typically someone a generation older. For Boomer-aged rabbis, the most frequently referenced rabbis were Abraham Joshua Heschel and Zalman Schachter-Shalomi. Gen X rabbis most often mentioned the influence of Rabbi Roly Matalon.[3]

While it is informative to learn which rabbis have most influenced their colleagues of different generations, more significant is a question these findings raise that requires further research, namely, to what extent does having a rebbe have an impact upon rabbinic leadership? I would suggest that this is an important variable in shaping rabbinic leadership. Leadership is often a heavy and lonely task. When rabbis view themselves as immediate disciples of someone with whom they have had a living and breathing relationship, they may derive the strength that is needed to remain tenaciously focused on a vision.

These rabbis also had other rebbes in a looser sense. In addition to being able to point to a specific influential rabbi, they were also able to point to at least one contemporary secular intellectual who had shaped their thinking on subjects such as the nature of community in a postmodern society and the search for a narrative that provides purpose for individuals and community. These rabbis we interviewed were substantive thinkers who validated our belief that American Jews are eager for intellectual depth in their rabbis, a quality that is not always displayed in congregations.

Obligation (*Hiyuv*) but Not Necessarily to the Whole System

The Hebrew word *hiyuv* literally means "obligation." Beyond its literal meaning, *hiyuv* signifies a broader belief in an entire system of Jewish law that rests on a belief in its divine origins (regardless of how the word *divine* is understood). Because Reform Judaism rejects the divine origins of Jewish law and views personal autonomy as the supreme determinant for individuals in deciding upon Jewish practice, it cannot use the language of *hiyuv* when describing its orientation toward Jewish law. Although Reconstructionist Judaism does not emphasize personal choice as the yardstick for determining Jewish practice as Reform Judaism does, Reconstructionist Judaism similarly rejects the divine origins of Jewish law. These views contrast with Conservative and Orthodox ideological stances toward Jewish law, in which the notion of *hiyuv*, of individuals being bound to an entire system of Jewish law, supersedes all other considerations when it comes to determining personal Jewish practice.[4]

Despite these significant distinctions in religious orientation, almost all the rabbis interviewed used the word *obligation* or *hiyuv* in describing their expectation that congregants will involve themselves in some aspect of Jewish life, whether it was study, prayer, service to the congregation or the community at large—or a combination of all these dimensions of Jewish life. While not all of the rabbis accepted the theological and all-encompassing legal aspects of the concept of *hiyuv*, they were at least comfortable in interpreting it to their congregants as applying to some area of Jewish life.

To be sure, many rabbis ask their members to commit to aspects of Jewish life from time to time. For example, rabbis typically ask their members to obligate themselves to a certain amount of daily or weekly study or to adopt a particular religious practice. But unlike typical rabbis who offer episodic pronouncements on the need for congregants to obligate themselves to Jewish practice, the rabbis we interviewed root their expectations of congregant obligation in a broader, systemic vision that they routinely promote. Thus, they are able to sustain a conversation about obligatory practice of ritual, prayer, or social justice. Just as these rabbis set the intellectual bar high for congregants, they also demonstrate that it is possible to create an expectation of congregant involvement in key aspects of Jewish life.

Risk Expected, Failure Embraced

The rabbis we interviewed all serve in congregations where both lay leaders and rabbis agree about the need to take risks and deviate from the "accepted way" things were done. One rabbi hyperbolically described his congregation's orientation toward experimentation as, "If it ain't broke, break it." These leaders were not enamored with innovation for its own sake, but they were not slaves to tradition and congregational culture. Several of them suggested that congregational leaders would feel disappointed if their synagogues did not experience periodic failure in trying new approaches.

Synagogues can be notoriously risk-averse. Congregational history, organizational culture, and an expectation of denominational conformity—all of these factors can weigh down a congregation's willingness and ability to change. Start-ups and younger congregations have an easier time with change, because they have no history that anchors them to traditions and because they benefit from the creative energy required to launch a new congregation. But we spoke with rabbis whose congregations were on many different stages of the organizational life span, including one whose congregation was more than 130 years old. Some rabbis had served their current congregations for only a few years, while others had celebrated long, milestone anniversaries. While only a few of the rabbis we interviewed were currently serving start-up congregations, every single one of them could be called a "start-up rabbi"—that is, one whose leadership has an entrepreneurial spirit.

Double Vision

Medically, double vision is defined as seeing two of everything, usually with one image partly obscuring the other. It is a physical condition that requires correction. From a leadership perspective, "double vision" is a condition that should be encouraged and nurtured. Many of the rabbis with whom we spoke were grounded in two cultures or world orientations. For example, one rabbi was steeped in Buddhism; another, psychology; a third, psychiatry; and still a fourth grew up outside the United States. To what extent does this double vision, this ability to bring two cultural frameworks to bear on a question or problem, contribute to innovation, creativity, and leadership? Without further study, it would be premature to conclude that rabbis who possess double vision are likely to be more effective congregational leaders. Nonetheless, this notion is worthy of further research, as it might suggest some direction to congregations when selecting a rabbi and to rabbis who want to develop their leadership abilities.

There is certainly intuitive wisdom in the idea that people who have lived for significant periods of times in two cultures have greater potential to become successful leaders. In some cases, these individuals may be able to analyze leadership challenges from different cultural perspectives and offer novel solutions that stem from the creative tension of dual perspectives. And, when we think generally about encounters with other people, which interactions tend to be more enriching—those with individuals who are monocultural or those who are bicultural; those who have limited life experiences or those who have cultivated a more variegated life?

The suggestion that people with more textured life experiences become more exceptional leaders aligns neatly with the journeys of some biblical leaders. For example, Moses brought two perspectives to his role as viceroy of Egypt. He was born a Hebrew but raised as an Egyptian. To the Egyptians, he was a Hebrew; to his Hebrew brothers, he appeared as an Egyptian. Perhaps this quality of double vision contributed to his leadership ability, enabling him to lead a group of humbled slaves and confront the unchallenged political leader of his day, Pharaoh. When we look at some of the great contemporary Jewish leaders such as Rabbis Heschel and Soloveitchik, we can observe how their hyphenated identities contributed to their religious creativity. Although each rabbi spent most of his active teaching years in America, both were born and raised in other countries and cultures and were steeped in rabbinic literature and secular philosophy.

The Role of Personal Theology in Congregational Life

One question we asked concerned the theology of the rabbis and its connection to their work: "Beyond ritual decisions, what role does your theology play in the work you do?" We also asked them how their theologies in the various structures of their organizations (for example, committees and boards) influenced their relationships with members, and how it was reflected in their programs.

With one exception, these rabbis were unable to make explicit connections between their personal theologies and the organizational structure of their congregations. We observed that many of these congregations seemed to be characterized by less hierarchy, which may have given them greater capacity for birthing new ideas. These rabbis practiced *tzitzum,* or a limitation of their leadership presence. Doing so enabled the talent within other staff members and congregants emerge.[5] Still, we were surprised these leaders had not given more thought to the relationship between personal theology and synagogue governance.

Evolution in Membership Structure

Generally speaking, most of the rabbis we interviewed are still working with a membership-dues model to finance congregational activities. In other words, members are expected to pay annual financial dues based on a "fair share" dollar amount that takes into account what the dues committee determines is reasonable for them to pay, relative to their earned income and that of other members of the congregation. The advantage to this model is that those who can pay more than their "fair share" financially support those who cannot pay dues or make only very modest payments. But, as noted in chapter 2, this model is highly problematic and not likely sustainable for most congregations.[6]

Some of the rabbis work in congregations that have made modifications to the standard financial-dues model. For example, some have expanded the concept of membership to include requirements of study, service to congregation and community, or personal involvement in the life of the congregation. Others within this group have dramatically reduced membership dues for younger adults. Still others have adjusted their expectations about the amount of money new members should have to pay within the first few years of membership. They recognized that in today's environment, expecting people to pay relatively steep membership dues immediately was shortsighted. Their approach was to charge nominal membership dues in the first few years and instead focus on developing relationships with new members through their involvement in the life of the community. Once the member had a history of positive involvement, someone from the congregation would have a conversation about an increased level of dues.

Finally, one congregation is in the early discussion stages of moving from a "culture of membership" to a "culture of philanthropy." Ultimately, the senior rabbi of this congregation would like to see mandatory dues replaced by a system of voluntary philanthropy. In other words, instead of having people view giving as an obligation (and perhaps thinking negatively about it), tap into their generosity and inspire them to want to give because the congregation does so much good for individuals, the Jewish community, and the broader civic and religious community.[7] The congregation's informal tests of this idea have brought positive preliminary feedback—which is not surprising, given that Chabad has used such an approach with great success.

Diversity Is Healthy

Another consistent theme we heard from these rabbis is the extent to which they cultivate diversity of perspectives and experiences among their members. This core value of diversity was manifested in different ways, depending upon the rabbi. For some, it meant endeavoring to present a range of religious views on current issues. Other rabbis routinely offered a wide gamut of programming so that congregants could express themselves Jewishly through study and social justice, in addition to prayer. A subset of these programmatically diverse rabbis made a point of explaining that by providing multiple experiences, they were making a statement that one type of Jewish experience was not superior to another. Study, social justice, prayer—each is an equally valid and valued way of committing to a Jewish life.

In several cases, rabbis described how their views on diversity were influenced by their college experiences at Hillel, a Jewish student organization on many college campuses whose mission statement explicitly mentions the values of pluralism and inclusion. Others referenced the influence of a teacher who modeled a strong commitment to pluralism. Regardless of the origins of their belief that diversity was a blessing, these rabbis do not take an "anything goes" stance that considers everything Jews do to be a Jewish experience. Rather, they promote an approach to Jewish living that extends an invitation to engage in a community with multiple entry points. They are confident in their own pattern of Jewish living, which gives them the ability to respect others who have different ways of living Jewishly.

Entrepreneurial Rabbis: An Emerging Category?

In researching this chapter, we stumbled upon a category of rabbis we had not considered previously. We call these rabbis "entrepreneurial rabbis," because they are deploying their rabbinic training and entrepreneurial personality to create a new kind of rabbinate outside the congregation and other venues in which rabbis have traditionally worked (for example, Jewish day schools, Jewish Community Centers, and Jewish camps). Of course, many innovative rabbis work within both congregations and these other settings. But their synagogues provide them with a regular income. By "entrepreneurial rabbis," we are referring to those who are not dependent at all or dependent only in part on congregational or institutional work for their income and have created a niche area of rabbinic work that does not fit neatly into any one existing model. Although we did not interview any of these rabbis, we want to call them to your attention, since we expect the phenomenon of rabbis who create their rabbinate outside congregations or Jewish organizations will become increasingly common in the American Jewish community.

Some of these entrepreneurial rabbis once worked in congregations but were forced by financial or political issues to seek new employment. Others made a conscious decision to create their rabbinate on their terms. They did not seek to develop a new organization with significant infrastructure. Rather, they essentially created their own small business.

The work these rabbis do varies greatly. Some have a passion for the outdoors, while others have an interest in technology. Still others use their knowledge of a specific area of Jewish law to create an income stream. As the number of synagogues in the United States contracts, it will be interesting to note whether this phenomenon expands. Additionally, if this phenomenon becomes more widespread, we will want to observe the extent to which it might affect the level of rabbinic entrepreneurship within congregations. As individuals have even more options for involvement in a spiritual community outside the current channels of congregations, will mainstream congregations grow more entrepreneurial in order to compete with these new expressions of Jewish life?

Missing a Framework for Jewish Spiritual Leadership

The rabbis we chose to interview were selected because each of them has rejected some of the premises of a twentieth-century synagogue and is consciously trying to create a more contemporary model of synagogue life within which Judaism can be expressed today. We chose rabbis who have reputations as catalysts and leaders of the movement toward synagogue change. Many of them have appeared in lists of "influential" rabbis.[8] Others have distinguished themselves through work in national congregational change initiatives or have been specially invited to participate in elite leadership development programs. Still others have led the way by the simple power of their own creativity and influenced congregations throughout the United States. While we already believed that these rabbis were inspiring leaders, after interviewing them, we were even more convinced of their exceptional leadership qualities.

As a byproduct of these interviews, I (Hayim) came to appreciate a stark fact: Although there are numerous rabbinical leadership programs, and most rabbinical schools now devote some attention to the nature of rabbinic leadership, the rabbinical world lacks systematic theories of rabbinic leadership development in which leadership programs can be anchored and assessed. I have worked professionally in the field of rabbinic leadership development since 1999 and have prior experience as a participant in some rabbinic leadership development programs. Also, through my volunteer involvement with the Alliance for Continuing Rabbinical Education,[9] I remain aware of the nature of most existing rabbinical leadership programs, and I believe they are not founded on leadership theory. Some programs incorporate a theory of change and may articulate the impact the program strives to have upon a rabbi and, in some cases, the intended impact that rabbis who participate in the program will have on their constituents. Other programs incorporate to varying degrees the concepts of highly respected academics who specialize in leadership development. However, as sound and valuable as these programs are, they embody ex post facto, implicit assumptions about how a rabbi is supposed to lead. For example, some programs assume that rabbis must intensify their personal spirituality or acquire knowledge of management skills to become more effective leaders. While these assumptions appear logical, we do not know if they have ever been tested. Because we lack more systematic theories of rabbinic leadership, those of us in this field often struggle to identify what program success looks like and how to measure it.

If we want to cultivate rabbinic leadership, it's time to develop some theory-based models. This is not a simple task, but it is feasible. Having been closely involved in designing a number of rabbinical leadership programs, I know that even designing a process to develop theory-based models of rabbinic leadership is a challenge. History, context, Jewish values, organizational values, understandings of the exercise of contemporary leadership and rabbinical leadership, including the role of gender, all have to be considered. But given how high the stakes are for rabbinical leaders and their ability to affect the tenor of Jewish life, it would be extremely worthwhile to begin this difficult task.

CHAPTER 6

You Have the Wisdom to Find the Way

Many books conclude with a summary list of tasks in which individuals or organizations can engage to experience renewal. By now, you already know that the complexities of the current state of synagogues make that kind of ending impossible. Certainly, there are strategies that can help your synagogue perform its current work better. But the purpose of this volume is to move synagogue leaders away from asking, "Are we doing the work right?" to "Are we doing the right work?" Do synagogues want to become better at doing work that seems to matter to fewer and fewer people with each passing year, or do they want to increase Jewish meaning and purpose for greater numbers of individuals?

Over the past fifteen years or so, I have generally observed two different trajectories among various experiments with synagogue change. The first approach suggests that the synagogue expression of Judaism may require some tinkering, but that it is fundamentally sound. We can call this line of thinking: "It's the people, not the product." The people just don't realize how much they are missing! If we could only get them to appreciate how much richer their lives could be, they would return to the synagogue. This approach results in various kinds of "campaigns": let's teach more Hebrew; let's offer better adult education; let's promote the values of eating kosher or observing Shabbat. These campaigns do tend to catch some individuals, but they have not resulted in systemic change.

The second approach to change acknowledges that all is not well within the synagogue walls. We can call this orientation, "It's the product, not the people." This thinking leads to changes that may include lowering membership dues for younger members; adding music to services; shortening the number of after-school educational "contact hours;" adding more variety to programming and services; or focusing more on the spiritual dimensions of synagogue life, such as prayer and study. Again, while these changes may increase the involvement of current members and draw in some new people, there is no evidence to suggest that this approach has dramatically improved American Jewish attitudes toward synagogues.

These two different approaches—(1) "It's the people, not the product," and (2) "It's the product, not the people"—have their roots in nineteenth-century Germany.[1] They share the assumption that synagogues are fundamentally doing "the right work"—they just have to do it better. The former approach was characteristic of neo-Orthodoxy, the latter of Reform Judaism. Both strategies enjoyed some success through the better part of the twentieth century. The neo-Orthodox approach resulted in the creation of a vibrant Orthodox community in the United States, which defied all predictions about the sustainability of Orthodoxy. Conservative, Reconstructionist, and Reform Judaism have provided a variety of robust Jewish alternatives to more complete assimilation into American culture. Both approaches have contributed to an exceptionally high quality of Jewish life in the United States, creating networks of synagogues, day schools, youth groups, camps, adult-learning programs, social-justice campaigns, and much more. But given the new realities synagogues face, these nineteenth-century strategies no longer address the challenges.

Beginning in the mid-1990s, foundations and philanthropists began to invest in national synagogue-transformation efforts, including the Koret Synagogue Initiative, Synagogue 2000/3000, ECE (The Experiment in Congregational Education), and STAR (Synagogues: Transformation and Renewal)—an initiative that I led. I believe that all of these efforts sincerely asked the question, "Are we doing the right work?" as they pursued their respective approaches to synagogue transformation. And all of them made vital conceptual and programmatic contributions to revitalizing synagogues. Nonetheless, even though we asked the right questions, we continued to operate on certain inherited assumptions about synagogues. I am suggesting that in this still relatively new century, we now need to question the synagogue's organizational fundamentals, beginning with mission, governance, and structure—something that, in my opinion, none of these earlier national transformation efforts did. Otherwise, synagogue thinking will remain anchored in a bygone era and will merely reiterate yesterday's attempts to solve today's spiritual, educational, and cultural issues.

Time to Reinvest in Synagogues

Retooling existing products and developing new ones require an infusion of different kinds of investments. The Jewish community has more than sufficient resources to reinvent existing synagogues, support promising emerging synagogue models, and develop innovative twenty-first-century synagogues. The real issue is whether those with the resources will recognize that vibrant, sustainable Jewish communities emerge when they are anchored in a strong religious core. Currently, it is the synagogue that primarily embodies the Jewish religious civilization. With a multipronged approach to investing in synagogues, philanthropic leaders will help to secure both synagogues and the many other nonreligious innovative initiatives they have developed.

Investing Funds in Synagogues

As a first step, synagogues need venture capital. Many start-up ventures rely on a handful of smaller investors, coincidentally called "angel investors." In the Bible angels are often portrayed as divine beings who appear at the exact moment someone is at a major crossroads.

A number of major philanthropists have invested in synagogues; without their support, national synagogue initiatives would never have occurred. But some philanthropists have concluded that synagogues cannot be changed or that the return does not justify the investment. My advice to those who think this way: Please reconsider your opinions and look again at the changes that have occurred through both your efforts and a handful of other efforts by farsighted federations like UJA-Federation of New York and the Combined Jewish Philanthropies of Boston. Reexamine your views in light of the future spiritual needs of the next generations of Jews who are in the early stages of adulthood. Invest in new models of synagogues that will speak more effectively to these generations.

There is also potential funding available for investing in new models of synagogues on the local level. In many congregations there are untapped financial angels who would be open to increasing their support, provided it promises a real turning point in the way the synagogue has functioned. Presented with the right opportunity, they will contribute financially. Combined with many administrative, technical, and educational resources that are either free or inexpensive, a little capital from angel investors can go a long way in revamping the organizational structure and culture of synagogues.

Investing in Leadership Excellence

But money is not the most important resource. If local philanthropists in every community decided to write personal checks tomorrow to close the budget deficits their synagogues are facing this year, many of those synagogues would be in the same predicament next year. Why? Because deeper organizational changes are needed, including assembling a team of lay and professional leaders that will bring fresh thinking, drive, and the courage to reenvision synagogue life.

In the business world, financial investors do not sink capital into a start-up enterprise with a mediocre leadership team, and we should not count on congregational supporters to do so either. The good news is that the talent pool in the Jewish community is exceptional. Synagogues need to capture more of that talent—which they can do if the stakes are higher than they usually are on synagogue boards and committees. I know too many potentially outstanding board members who have been driven away by boards that focus too much time and energy on operational issues and not nearly enough on vision, Jewish meaning, goals, and policies—the kinds of issues that really belong in the purview of governing boards. A chronic shortage of funds is a serious issue in synagogues, but money is never a substitute for dreams, imagination, inspiration, and excellence in executing ideas.

That is why I also encourage national and local philanthropists to invest in new models of lay-leadership development for synagogues. National philanthropists could create collaborative, cross-denominational programs to develop synagogue leaders who have a global perspective on the synagogue and Jewish life, while local Jewish communities could sponsor collaborative synagogue lay-leadership development programs that focus on the particular issues of a community. One model for synagogue collaboration is the Wexner Heritage Program, a collaborative community-leadership program that brings a diverse group of young leaders together to prepare them to lead major local Jewish community organizations.[2] Based on the success of the Wexner Heritage Program, there are good reasons to adapt that model to synagogue leadership programs by creating an invitation-only program of the most creative and innovative young lay leaders who have expressed a commitment to synagogues.

On both the national and local levels, the content of this initiative would not be about the nuts-and-bolts of running a congregation. Rather, it would focus on helping synagogues reorient their mission and reengineer their processes to a twenty-first-century Jewish community. This kind of program would foster a cross-pollination of the most thoughtful and electrifying thinking about how to redesign synagogues regardless of denominational affiliation.

It would be difficult for any one synagogue to create this kind of high-level program on its own, but such an effort is financially feasible when created collaboratively. Synagogue staff members could still provide individualized training for their lay leaders, teaching them about the specific issues of their respective congregations. If we really want to dream, denominational movements could help fund these programs and serve as clearinghouses for program-related resources.

Investing in Continuing Rabbinic Education

Continuing rabbinical education (CRE)—and, for that matter, continuing education for all synagogue professionals—is a necessity. Some synagogues are diligent about ensuring that their rabbis participate in some CRE experience annually, in addition to attending their rabbinical conventions. However, the level of congregational support for continuing education, especially in these stressful financial times, is uneven. In contrast, at least until the recent economic crunch, within the Protestant world it has been customary for clergy members to have one to two weeks of required continuing education annually, which is not counted as vacation and for which the congregation commits a set amount of money.[3]

Why is CRE so important? If you learned that your physician's medical education ended after graduation twenty years ago and that his license had expired because of a failure to accumulate continuing education credits, how soon would you be looking for a new doctor? Of course, you want a doctor who keeps abreast of current research, learns new skills, and refreshes long-standing ones. Why should we expect any less of rabbis, given the gravity of the work they do? In an ideal world, seminaries or rabbinical organizations would issue licenses that would allow rabbis to continue practicing only if they'd taken a set amount of continuing education credits in the past three to five years.

Investing in Teaching Synagogues

Rabbi Roly Matalon of B'nai Jeshurun in Manhattan and Rabbi Jonathan Rosenblatt of Riverdale Jewish Center in the Bronx introduced me to the concept of a teaching synagogue during my interviews with them. Although their efforts differ in implementation, each of these rabbis has created a fellowship or internship program at his synagogue that is modeled after a teaching hospital. Teaching hospitals are typically associated with universities and engaged in educational and research programs. The association with a university allows the hospital to provide clinical care based on best practices rooted in research and innovative and experimental care.

The internships Rabbis Matalon and Rosenblatt have developed provide rabbinical students and early-career rabbis opportunities to experience congregational life with the benefit of a proven mentor-innovator. These rabbinic interns can enjoy the best of all worlds. They can experiment boldly but the mentor rabbi provides a shield from negative congregational fallout if a new program or process goes awry. When these interns lead their own congregations, they will begin with a base of knowledge and experience and a network of support of other interns and a mentor rabbi. With these advantages, these young rabbis will have a greater likelihood of developing more vibrant synagogues.

Denominational leaders and independent synagogues should consider adapting the concept of teaching hospitals to synagogues. The teaching synagogue would supply the clinical experience, and seminary faculty would contribute their expertise in research, helping synagogues develop model practices and collaborating with the synagogues in researching innovation. The cost of creating teaching synagogues could be shared between the synagogue itself, which benefits from having rabbinic fellows, and its national denominational organization. In return for its support, the denomination could then require all fellows to serve the congregations of its choice for a two-year period. Additionally, the movements would reap the rewards of training young rabbis with the most exemplary rabbinic leaders. Over a relatively brief period of time, the impact of teaching synagogues could be substantial, and the positive effect could multiply over decades if teaching fellows formed networks where they would continue to exchange ideas and experiences. I have included a more detailed description of the respective models of teaching synagogues of Rabbi Matalon and Rabbi Rosenblatt in their own words below, as they merit further exploration and replication.

Rabbi Roly Matalon

Congregation B'nai Jeshurun, New York, New York

In 1996, B'nai Jeshurun (BJ) created the Marshall T. Meyer Rabbinic Fellowship, a two-year rabbinic apprenticeship open to students from any of the accredited rabbinical schools. The first year of the fellowship was a part-time position for approximately ten hours per week, a schedule suited to the fellow's last year in school. Upon ordination, the fellow began work at BJ full-time for one year.

As of this year, the BJ Rabbinic Fellowship has been reconfigured as a one-year, twenty-hours-per-week program for students who have completed at least two years of rabbinical school. The fellowship is dedicated to understanding how BJ functions, meeting key players in the community (such as board members, chairs of committees, and staff), creating a relationship of trust with the rabbis, being present at certain pastoral rabbinic situations, and taking on responsibilities within the community.

The fellows engage in ongoing learning and supervision. Their general responsibilities include having a weekly ninety-minute meeting with the rabbis, teaching a weekly class on *Parashat Hashavua* (the weekly Torah portion) or Introduction to Judaism, leading morning minyan, working with conversion candidates, leading prayers at a house of mourning, periodic leadership of Shabbat services, including delivering *divrei torah* (sermons), and supporting the rabbinic department in various ways (including research, production of materials, and programmatic responsibilities).

Upon completion of the fellowship, the fellows participate in an annual retreat with all current and alumni fellows to provide an opportunity to maintain the relationships of the past, create a support system for the future for rabbis who have internalized the philosophy and vision of BJ, and offer a moment of spiritual renewal.

BJ Rabbinic fellowship alumni presently serve in congregations and Hillels across the United States and Israel. The leaders and members of the BJ community feel privileged that our congregation can serve as a mentoring institution for future spiritual leaders of the Jewish people.

Rabbi Jonathan Rosenblatt
Riverdale Jewish Center, New York, New York

In the year 2000 I resigned from my synagogue to pursue a personal passion: the training of young rabbis, with an emphasis on the art of the leader as shepherd. Rabbis who see themselves as shepherds view all their work as an outgrowth of the pastoral role, a function of their relationships. This pastoral role subsumes the roles of teacher, visionary, and builder. A committee of the board of trustees asked me to reconsider my resignation. Their offer: Do the work you had hoped to do outside our congregation within the Riverdale Jewish Center (RJC). Learning that I could fulfill my own vision as a rabbi within my congregation was a seminal lesson for me.

Shortly thereafter, I hired the first rabbinic intern, and the RJC subsequently has had four or five interns on average each year. Altogether, some thirty young men, all of whom were learned, devout, and talented before they crossed my threshold, have come to the RJC to learn the *craft* of the community rabbi. The RJC is a multigenerational, multidimensional synagogue community. It has several minyanim (prayer services), each with a unique character, and an active youth community. The RJC has a diverse membership: young couples, titans of industry, Holocaust survivors, elders, academics, and Torah scholars. Given its diversity, the RJC is a multiplex of life stages that are intimate and public, intellectual and emotional, joyous and catastrophic.

The concept of the Teaching Shul (synagogue) was to use these "stages" as a way to provide a full range of rabbinic functions. The interns preach, teach, give *Halachic* (legal) guidance, tackle administrative challenges, and comfort the ill and the bereaved. I, together with the executive director, assistant rabbi, and the *chazzan* (cantor), mentor and supervise the interns and shield them from significant political pressures.

Interns generally serve for two years and become "senior interns" with more administrative and programmatic responsibility during the second year. In addition to shadowing opportunities and many Shabbatot around my family's table, each intern meets privately with me each week. The interns determine how to use this time, whether for homiletic consultation, personal issues, faith-related discussions, or professional guidance. It is their time.

Referred to as "the Rabbinic Team" or just "the Team," the interns, the assistant rabbi, and I meet weekly together to distribute responsibilities, evaluate programs, and chart the future. In that meeting, everyone is expected to be candid and creative; hierarchy is largely abandoned. "The Team" runs the sacred dimension of the synagogue, thus distinguishing our approach from internships that are more limited in scope. I believe that rabbis trained in a team approach will develop over time into more trusting and cooperative colleagues.

What has occurred in the course of the decade of the Intern Initiative is a shift in our congregational structure. The members and leadership of the RJC have come to see the training of young rabbis as part of the synagogue's core mission. Each fall, the arrival of the new interns is a major event; their company at Shabbat tables is often a hot ticket. Within a month the congregational pundits are predicting which ones are headed for greatness and which ones need work. And when former interns return for visits, they are embraced and welcomed with great pride.

Perhaps the greatest testament to the Intern Initiative is that the past three assistant rabbis have been chosen from among our senior interns and that now each assistant rabbi is obligated by contract "to assist in the coordination of rabbinic interns." Once *I* had a vision that a large mainstream congregation could be used as a training platform for new rabbis; now the *members and leaders* of the community define their synagogue as a Teaching Shul.

Investing in Collaboration

The challenges of local collaboration on the synagogue level that I discussed in chapter 3 have parallels on the national level. The most significant barrier to collaboration is a fear of loss of constituent members to "competitor" movements. Admittedly, national synagogue leaders, like leaders of all national organizations, face a difficult time. Increasingly, affiliates of such organizations are asking whether the cost of belonging is worth the value of membership. Given the pervasive availability of free or inexpensive programmatic, educational, and administrative resources, how can member affiliates justify paying as much as they do in membership dues for the services they receive? That question creates understandable pressure for national organizations to demonstrate the value of being a dues-paying constituent. This dynamic does not foster a spirit of cross-organizational collaboration, as national organizations understandably are more concerned with serving their respective members than sharing with "competitor" movements.

Yet, synagogues will be so much more effective and dynamic if the national denominations model collaboration. Those who work on the national level understand better than anyone that stronger synagogues contribute to more vibrant Jewish communities; therefore, these leaders have a great stake in helping all synagogues become more relevant. If some synagogues are perceived as weak, the public's impression of all synagogues will be negatively affected. But if synagogues are considered centers of Jewish creativity, they have the potential to power the Jewish community in North America toward a renaissance of Jewish life.

These collaborative efforts could be focused initially around neutral issues, such as practices in administration, management, Hebrew language education, and other key aspects of synagogue life. In an age where there are few secrets and individual congregations in the same city learn from one another anyway, the national movements could, for example, start a collaborative journal dedicated to exemplary synagogue life. Such a step would offer helpful strategic and programmatic support to all synagogues while also sending a symbolic message that would encourage local congregations of different denominations to collaborate more effectively. Equally important, a cross-denominational journal could help synagogues circumvent mistakes by highlighting failed experiments that are instructive for future pilot efforts.

Finally, while synagogues and denominations often think in terms of "their" members or potential members, we know that people today are mobile. They are willing to switch from one denomination to another within their community, and if they move to another city, they may choose to affiliate with a different denomination. Given this mobility, national leaders have a vested interest in helping make sure that wherever people's spiritual journeys take them, they will find a synagogue that is compatible with their spiritual temperaments.

Investing in Tomorrow's Synagogue Today

You do not have to wait for changes on the national level in order to begin developing the synagogue of the future. In fact, no one will do it for you. As my friends and colleagues Rabbi Terry Bookman and Dr. Bill Kahn of Eitzah remind their clients, the answers to the question "What does a group need?" usually exist within the group itself.[4] I would add only that this observation is true if the group is honest in assessing its needs.

Expert consultants can provide resources, tools, and insights and can help a group frame questions, test assumptions, and refine potential solutions. If a group is honest and courageous, it can use its collective wisdom to generate paradigm-shifting ideas.

To get started, congregations only have to be willing to change their conversations about the essential purposes of a twenty-first-century synagogue.

For an illustration, let's look at a very challenging issue: prayer. In liberal congregations, prayer services are often highly problematic. If you are reading this book, you're probably already aware of the litany of complaints leveled against synagogue prayer services: too long, too inaccessible because of the amount of Hebrew language, and insufficiently engaging. One primary task of the synagogue is to help people develop a relationship with God and the Jewish community through prayer. No other Jewish institution has that task as a part of its mission. Given the synagogue's general lack of success in achieving this core part of its mission, rabbis and concerned volunteer leaders often have conversations about prayer. Some of the discussion strands I hear from congregational leaders around the desire to engage more congregants in prayer are:

- "We need to have better music in services."
- "Services are too long. How can we shorten them?"
- "Services need to be more participatory; we need more singing."
- "There's too much/too little Hebrew in services. We should remove/add some Hebrew passages."

These observations may help ritual committees generate some welcome modifications for those who are generally satisfied with how services are already run. But such ideas are simply more tinkering at the temple, because they presume the existing framework of prayer services provides an adequate response to contemporary spiritual issues. The kinds of discussions I encourage people to have begin with the assumption that prayer as expressed in most liberal synagogues does not work for the majority of the Jewish community. We know this from low participation rates in synagogue services. Here are some sample questions that can open up possibilities for fundamentally changing the experience of prayer services:

- Do people who define themselves as "secular" believe God listens to their prayers? (There is research that suggests they do.[5]) Would any kinds of prayer experiences interest them? If so, why has Humanistic Judaism, which removes God from its liturgy, attracted so little interest?
- What can U.S. synagogues learn from the phenomenon of "secular services" that have developed in Israel?
- Are any parts of the liturgy off limits when working on revitalizing prayer, or is everything up for discussion?
- American Jews find spiritual fulfillment outside Judaism, in spirituality and meditation centers. Do we know what aspects of those experiences they find most compelling? Would it be beneficial to incorporate more of those aspects into prayer services? Should synagogues and local meditation centers offer joint prayer services?
- Should the Jewish community partner more frequently with churches to create ecumenical services, like the kind that occur on Thanksgiving or Memorial Day?
- How might we build national and global synagogue prayer partnerships where, for example, a congregation in Jerusalem and a congregation in Minneapolis might join together to plan and then simultaneously videocast services?
- What images of God resonate for people today, and how do these images compare and contrast with the images of God found in existing Jewish liturgies?
- To what extent do existing liturgies, even when offered in accessible translations, speak to people today? What is usable from the past, and what may have run its course?

- What can we learn about the experience of prayer from other faith traditions in order to make Jewish prayer more enriching?
- What do people who have difficulty with existing liturgies hope to experience if they could find a way to pray?
- How have other religious traditions grappled with these questions?

Every congregation has thoughtful, creative, and imaginative leaders who can formulate essential questions like these. Asking such questions repeatedly and experimenting with answers will put your congregation on a path toward a paradigm shift in prayer.

Remember: Those who enjoy prayer as it is expressed currently in the synagogue should not have to give up their experience! The idea is to add to the repertoire of experiences in a congregation, without disenfranchising those who like it the way it is. If a congregation believes it is too small to begin a discussion that might lead to an alternative prayer option, it can collaborate with another congregation. If congregations are willing to honestly and courageously initiate these discussions and allow them to run their course, they generate fruitful ideas and experiences that will invite many more people into an authentic experience of personal and congregational prayer. Some experiments will fail, but failure, as much as success, will stimulate innovation, learning, excitement, and engagement with all kinds of congregants and seekers who are dissatisfied with the current expressions of prayer. Indeed, the primary task of synagogue leaders today is to ask essential questions that have the potential to realign synagogues to the twenty-first-century realities I have described in this book.

The rabbis I interviewed for chapter 5 inspired me with their love of Judaism and their belief in its enduring ability to develop Jewishly educated, spiritual, and compassionate people—people who look beyond their own growth and contribute to making a more just world for all. If you are a part of a synagogue community, you likely share some of these same hopes. You do not have to become like one of these rabbis to begin to transform your own congregation. You just have to be courageous enough to become more of yourself. Each rabbi in these interviews left me reflecting on an especially memorable insight. I pass on their wisdom with the hope that they will enable you to more confidently exercise your own authentic leadership.

- "Every time we have Shabbat together, people start from their place of pain, loss, longing, or fear, and then they recognize at some point . . . that they are in the room with hundreds of people who are having very different experiences. You are forced to understand that your experience of the world isn't the only thing that's happening. Together, we can work for the transformation of the city and the world in some way" (Rabbi Sharon Brous).
- "Every day you have to be learning how to live—that's what *halacha* is. *Halacha* is simply the road map in the texts of a considered life, at every moment of life for the entire path of life" (Rabbi Danny Zemel).
- "The name of community (Kavana Cooperative), and its goal, is to push people to think about decisions in their lives in intentional ways" (Rabbi Rachel Nussbaum).
- "B'nai Jeshurun is a very Heschelian congregation. We see ourselves as having to respond to being given the privilege of life and being in God's presence. God's question is *ayekah.*[6] Now, how do I respond? That is at the basis of our theology" (Rabbi Roly Matalon).
- "Judaism is a powerful, spiritual tool. Judaism is one of the many systems that the planet has produced to create greater human beings. The synagogue should be a courageous outpost that allows people to do the exercises that will help keep the soul in shape" (Rabbi David Ingber).

- "Our address is our mission and vision and not just our geographic location" (Rabbi Marcia Zimmerman).
- "Judaism should be compelling but not coercive" (Rabbi Mikki Rosenberg).
- "Judaism is about growth and movement *(lekh l'ekha),* and that growth is found to a great extent in diversity and hearing different voices" (Rabbi Asher Lopatin).
- "A rabbi is not a solo actor but a producer and director who enables others to take the stage" (Rabbi Jonathan Rosenblatt).
- "If you really want numbers, make yourselves more relevant" (Rabbi Tirza Firestone).

I have been blessed with the opportunity to work with hundreds of rabbis and other synagogue leaders over the years, and I have been equally moved by your wisdom about Jewish life. You, too, have the wisdom to help others find their way through these turbulent times if you will have the courage and faith to claim a greater role as leaders. "Hope in *Adonai*. Be strong and courageous, and hope in *Adonai*" (Ps. 27:14).

Notes

Introduction

1. For example, see Isa Aron, et al., *A Congregation of Learners: Transforming the Synagogue into a Learning Community* (New York: UAHC Press, 1995); Aron et al., *Sacred Strategies: Transforming Synagogues from Functional to Visionary* (Herndon, VA: Alban Institute, 2010); Zachary I. Heller, *Re-Envisioning the Synagogue*. (Newton, MA: National Center for Jewish Policy Studies at Hebrew College, 2005); Heller, *Synagogues in a Time of Change: Fragmentation and Diversity in Jewish Religious Movements* (Herndon, VA: Alban Institute, 2009); Sid Schwarz, *Finding a Spiritual Home: How a New Generation of Jews Can Transform the American Synagogue* (San Francisco: Jossey-Bass, 2000); and David Teutsch, *Spiritual Community: The Power to Restore Hope, Commitment and Joy* (Woodstock, VT: Jewish Lights Publishing, 2005).
2. Some publications examine newer, more fundamentally different models of organization and governance of independent minyanim. For example, see Elie Kaunfer, *Empowered Judaism: What Independent Minyanim Can Teach Us about Building Vibrant Jewish Communities* (Woodstock, VT: Jewish Lights Publishing, 2010).
3. www.joelbarker.com.

Chapter 2: Exploring a Twenty-First-Century Synagogue

1. See Chris Anderson, *Free: The Future of a Radical Price* (New York: Hyperion, 2009); Anderson, *The Long Tail: Why the Future of Business Is Selling Less of More* (New York: Hyperion, 2006); Allison Fine and Beth Kanter, *The Networked Nonprofit: Connecting with Social Media to Drive Change* (San Francisco: John Wiley and Sons, 2010); Jeff Jarvis, *What Would Google Do?* (New York: HarperCollins, 2009); and Charlene Li, *Open Leadership: How Social Technology Can Transform the Way You Lead* (San Francisco: Jossey-Bass, 2010).
2. I understand the skepticism some people have about the value of mission statements. That skepticism is often the result of spending a significant amount of time crafting one, only to discover that it has had no impact on an organization. For a strong case on the value of mission statements, see David A. Teutsch, *Making a Difference: A Guide to Jewish Leadership and Not-for-Profit Management* (Philadelphia: Reconstructionist Rabbinical College Press, 2009), 81. Teutsch writes, "A strong organization both articulates a picture of the world it is attempting to create and its own particular role in creating it. Any mission answers the question, why do you exist as an organization? You can also think of a mission statement as a tombstone. If your congregation was to leave this world, what epitaph would people write about it?" When your mission statement becomes the touchstone for decisionmaking in your congregation, it will maximize the impact that your congregation will have in the world.
3. Written communication with Professor Joe Magee, Associate Professor of Management, New York University, Wagner Graduate School of Public Service, February 11, 2011.
4. For more information on best board practices, see Richard P. Chait et al., *Governance as Leadership: Reframing the Work of Boards* (Hoboken, NJ: John Wiley and Sons, 2005), and

John Carver, *Boards That Make a Difference: A New Design for Leadership in Nonprofit and Public Organizations*, 3rd ed. (San Francisco: Jossey-Bass, 2006). Also see Compass Point Nonprofit Services (www.compasspoint.org) and Board Source (www.boardsource.org) for online resources. Additionally, the Alban Institute (www.alban.org) has a significant number of publications on church and synagogue governance.

5. I have heard Jill use this phrase in many of her presentations, and I acknowledge her as the source for much that I have learned about volunteer engagement. You can learn more about her work at http://www.jffixler.com/category/blog-tags/jill-friedman-fixler.
6. Gary Tobin, "Will the Synagogue Survive?" *Moment Magazine*, August 1991, 44–49.
7. Jonathan Woocher, *If You Build It, Will They Come? Accessibility, Affordability, and Participation in Jewish Communal Life* (Los Angeles: University of Judaism, The Center for Policy Options, 1999).
8. For a detailed discussion on attitudes of Jewish Baby Boomers toward "encore" careers in Jewish communal service and for subsequent policy recommendations, see David Elcott, "Baby Boomers, Public Service, and Minority Communities: A Case Study of the Jewish Community in the United States." Berman Jewish Policy Archive, Research Center for Leadership in Action, NYU Wagner (2010). http://www.bjpa.org/Publications/details.cfm?PublicationID=5154.
9. Alice Mann, *The In-Between Church: Navigating Size Transitions in Congregations*. (Bethesda, MD: Alban Institute, 1998), 42–43.

Chapter 3: The Case for Collaboration

1. The exception to this general rule is in interfaith partnerships with local churches and, increasingly, mosques.

2. See David La Piana, "Strategic Restructuring: Partnership Options for Nonprofits," La Piana Consulting, January 4, 2011, http://www.La Piana.org/strategic-restructuring.
3. For the definitive work on the subject of networks and nonprofits, see Beth Kanter and Allison H. Fine, *The Networked Nonprofit: Connecting with Social Media to Drive Change* (San Francisco: Jossey-Bass, 2010).
4. For a comparison of local Jewish communities in the United States, see Ira M. Sheskin, *How Jewish Communities Differ* (Storrs, CT: North American Jewish Data Bank, 2001).
5. For a more detailed discussion of narrowing differences among liberal denominations, see Hayim Herring, "Synagogue Renewal in an Age of Extreme Choice: Anything, Anyone, Anytime, Anywhere," *Synagogues in a Time of Change*, ed. Zachary I. Heller (Herndon, VA: Alban Institute, 2009), 125–30.

Chapter 4: Remixing the Rabbinate

1. See "Rabbinate," *Encyclopedia Judaica* (Jerusalem, Israel: Keter Publishing House, 1971), columns 1445–58.
2. Talmud Bavli, Berakhot 31a.
3. Talmud Bavli, Pesachim 113b.
4. Talmud Bavli, Gittin 67b.
5. Talmud Bavli, Megillah 28b.
6. See "Rabbinate" and David Star, *A World within a World: The History of the Modern Synagogue," Re-envisioning the Synagogue*, ed. Zachary I. Heller (Boston, MA: National Center for Jewish Policy Studies and STAR [Synagogues: Transformation and Renewal], 2005) 44–49.
7. "Rates of Intermarriage," *National Jewish Population Survey (NJPS) 2000–2001*, Sept. 2003, http://www.jewishfederations.org/page.aspx?id=46253.

8. "NJPS: The Elderly," *NJPS 2000–2001,* January 21, 2011, http://www.jewishfederations.org/page.aspx?id=45896.
9. For a recent and authoritative study on this issue, see Steven M. Cohen and Laura Blitzer, *Belonging without Believing: Jews and Their Distinctive Patterns of Religiosity—and Secularity* (New York: Florence G. Heller-JCC Association [JCCA] Research Center, 2008). The study, based on the 2008 Pew Forum U.S. Religious Landscape Survey, found that compared to Evangelicals, mainstream Protestants, and Catholics, "Jews uniformly score lower . . . on all available measures of religious belief." For example, religion is "very important" to only 31 percent of Jews, significantly less than the three other groups.
10. For an in-depth discussion on religion in American life, see Robert Putnam and David Campbell, *American Grace* (New York: Simon and Schuster, 2010).
11. Cohen and Blitzer, 15.
12. As a limited list, Rabbis Akiva and Yohanan in the Rabbinic Period; throughout the Medieval Period, Maimonides, Rabbi Isaac Luria, and the Baal Shem Tov; and in the Modern Period, Rabbis Israel Salanter, Shimshon Rafael Hirsch, Abraham Isaac Kook, Abraham Joshua Heschel, Joseph Soloveitchik, Mordechai Kaplan, the Lubavitcher Rebbe and Rabbi Zalman Schachter-Shalomi.
13. For an excellent anthology of the impact of rabbinic and other kinds of spiritual leadership on Jewish communities throughout the ages, see Jack Wertheimer, ed., *Jewish Religious Leadership: Image and Reality* (New York: Jewish Theological Seminary of America, 2004).
14. "The Jewish Innovation Economy," *Jumpstart,* April 2011, 14–16.
15. A version of this section first appeared in "Passion Yes, Charisma No," *Shma: A Journal of Jewish Responsibility,* March 2009, 10–11.

16. Anya Kamenetz, "A Is for App: How Smartphones, Handheld Computers Sparked an Educational Revolution," *Fast Company,* April 2010, April 22, 2011, http://www.fastcompany.com/magazine/144/a-is-for-app.html.
17. For more on this topic, see my articled entitled "The Rabbi as *Moreh Derekh Chayim*: Reconceptualizing Today's Rabbinate," *CCAR: A Reform Jewish Quarterly,* Winter 2006, 49–58.
18. Talmud Bavli, Avodah Zarah 35b.
19. David E. Kaufman "The Synagogue as a Mediating Institution," *Re-envisioning the Synagogue,* ed. Zachary I. Heller (Herndon, VA: Alban Institute, 2005) 3–37.
20. See www.aish.com for a number of examples.
21. I want to acknowledge my colleague Karen Sobel for formulating the importance of innovation in this particular way.

Chapter 5: Pathways to Synagogues of the Future

1. Avi Herring, a graduate student in NYU's dual-degree program between the Wagner School of Public Service and the Skirball Department of Hebrew and Judaic Studies, assisted with the interviews and coauthored the chapter with me.
2. Rabbis interviewed were Sharon Brous (IKAR, Los Angeles), Tirzah Firestone (Nevei Kodesh, Boulder, CO), David Ingber (Romemu, New York), Asher Lopatin (Anshe Sholom, Chicago), Roly Matalon (B'nai Jeshurun, New York), Rachel Nussbaum (Kavanah Cooperative, Seattle), Michaël Rosenberg (Fort Tryon Jewish Center, New York), Jonathan Rosenblatt (Riverdale Jewish Center, New York), Danny Zemel (Temple Micah, Washington, DC), Marcia Zimmerman (Temple Israel, Minneapolis). We also interviewed a number of independent minyanim and congregations that were not led by rabbis or governed by a volunteer council that included rabbis. However, we found that the directors of these synagogues and minyanim were unable to respond to questions about theology and

mission. They were only able to speak about their programs and their constituents.

3. Rabbi Abraham Joshua Heschel was a prominent theologian and civil rights activist at the Jewish Theological Seminary; Rabbi Zalman Schachter-Shalomi is the founder of the Jewish Renewal Movement; Rabbi Roly Matalon is senior rabbi at Congregation B'nai Jeshurun and one of the interviewees in this book. Rabbi Lopatin and Rabbi Rosenblatt each cited different mentor rabbis, but each spoke about their respective mentors as models of rabbis who used their influence to empower people and not constrain them.
4. The fact that the overwhelming majority of Jews who affiliate as Conservative do not actually believe in the divine origins of an encompassing system of Jewish law does not invalidate this distinction between Conservative Judaism, on the one hand, and Reconstructionist and Reform Judaism on the other.
5. See Eugene B. Borowitz, *Exploring Jewish Ethics: Papers on Covenant Responsibility* (Detroit: Wayne State University Press, 1990) 320–31.
6. "The Cost of Belonging," *The Jewish Daily Forward,* September 7, 2010, http://www.forward.com/articles/131095/.
7. The senior rabbi is Rabbi Marcia Zimmerman of Temple Israel in Minneapolis.
8. These lists appear in publications including *Newsweek* and *The Jewish Daily Forward.*
9. For more information, visit allianceforcre.org.

Chapter 6: You Have the Wisdom to Find the Way

1. Steven Lowenstein, *Old Orthodox and Neo-Orthodox Rabbinic Responses to the Challenges of Modernity in Nineteenth-century Germany,* vol. 2, in *Jewish Religious Leadership: Image and Reality,* edited by Jack Wertheimer, 481–503 (New York: Jewish Theological Seminary, 2004).

2. The Wexner Foundation, "Wexner Heritage Program: Mission/History," http://www.wexnerfoundation.org/WexnerHeritageProgram/MissionHistory/tabid/76/Default.aspx.
3. Larry Goleman, "2008 Conference Materials," *Alliance for Continuing Rabbinic Education,* July 24, 2009, http://allianceforcre.org/component/docman/doc_download/15-criteria-and-evaluation-of-clergy-continuing-education.
4. Eitzah: Center for Congregational Leadership. *About Us.* http://eitzah.org/about.html.
5. Egon Mayer, Barry A. Kosmin, and Ariela Keysar, *American Jewish Identity Survey Report: An Exploration in the Demography and Outlook of a People* (Survey, NY: Graduate Center of the City University of New York, 2001), Exhibit 12, 39–40.
6. The Hebrew word *ayekah* literally means "Where are you?," the question that God asks Adam in Genesis 3:9 when he tries to hide from the presence of God.